MASS SHOOTINGS

Six Steps to Survival

4th Edition

John Matthews

Mass Shootings: Six Steps to Survival (4th Ed.)

CSI Publishing, Dallas, Texas.

ISBN 978-0-9888556-6-3

Contents

INTRODUCTION

We have all seen the shocking and heart-wrenching news accounts from places we might have never before heard of, but which are now forever burned into our American collective consciousness. Mention San Bernardino or the "Batman" shooting, Virginia Tech, the Pulse nightclub in Orlando, or the attack on Congresswoman Gabrielle Giffords, and immediately our minds flash to news footage of carnage and chaos as we mentally replay the images of so many innocent victims. Who is ever going to forget the five police officers murdered ambush-style that hot July night in Dallas? Perhaps the most mind-numbing of all was the 2012 tragedy in Newtown, Connecticut, where 20 elementary-school-aged children and six of their teachers were killed at Sandy Hook Elementary School —and then came the October 2017 Route 91 Harvest Festival massacre in Las Vegas, where 58 people lost their lives and more than 1200 were wounded by gunfire or suffered other injuries in the attack. Valentine's Day of 2018 saw yet another school shooting in Parkland, Florida, where 17 students and teachers were killed and another 16 wounded.

When news accounts of these attacks first hit our airwaves, our first question is usually WHY? Why did such a terrible event have to occur? Why would someone randomly take the lives of innocent people?

Throughout the country, in homes, offices, and restaurants, we stay glued to our favorite source of news and information. Whether from radio or television, from news reports viewed on our computer or cellphone screens, from constant streams of Facebook posts or by Twitter updates, we seek answers. As details of the event begin to emerge, and pieces of the puzzle begin to fit together, eventually many of our questions regarding the attack are answered. We usually discover in fairly short time the *who, what, where, when* and *how*—sometimes even the *why* or the motive for the attack—but for many of us, one question always lurks in the back of our consciousness:

What would I do if I were ever involved in a mass shooting? As we ask that question, and as we run through various scenarios in our minds, we soon discover that we have questions we can't answer:

How would I respond to a heavily-armed gunman who is determined to kill as many people as possible? What would I do if I were caught in the wrong place at the wrong time: in a crowded movie theater, at a popular concert, out celebrating at a city festival, or simply eating lunch with my child at school?

What do I do? *Do I have the knowledge and skills necessary to survive an attack? How do I save myself and help others?*

All these questions and more are answered in *Mass Shootings: Six Steps to Survival*, a book written specifically to give everyone the information and tools necessary to survive a mass shooting or active shooter assault.

Examining nearly 80 mass shootings that have occurred in the United States since 1980, this book focuses on the actions taken and the decisions made by those who survived these horrific attacks, as well as lessons learned from those who did not survive. Armed with this new information, the old axiom "fight or flight" is dispelled—or at least modified—regarding this new breed of killer. Fight by yourself, and you are almost certainly going to join the ranks of the victims, if not the overall body count; attempt to flee and present a target for the killer or draw his attention, and the chances are you will not make it out alive.

Designed as a compendium of lessons learned, this book offers vital information gleaned from the survivors who have successfully endured some of the most tragic and violent incidents in U.S. history. Neither condemning nor condoning such actions, but simply presenting and analyzing the data, has allowed this author to both glean unique observations of strategies and tactics employed, and develop a teachable model to use to improve one's chances of successfully surviving a mass shooting.

So what are your chances of being involved in a mass shooting? And how does one define this phenomenon? Traditionally, the Federal Bureau of Investigation (FBI) defined a mass shooting as an incident in which *four or more* people (not including the perpetrator) are killed in a single event. In 2013, Congress enacted Public Law 112-265 qualifying a mass killing as one where three or more victims die in a single incident, significantly altering the total count of mass shootings which have occurred in the United States. To maintain research consistency, the traditional FBI definition of mass shooting is utilized; thus, for purposes of this book, our definition of a mass shooting is:

- four or more persons killed (not including the perpetrator)
- using firearms
- in a continuing incident
- involving a public place

Although there is a nexus between domestic and family violence, with a significant number of mass shooters killing family members, our definition of mass shootings does not include instances of domestic violence where the crimes were committed solely in private residences. This definition also does not include murders that occurred during the commission of another crime such as a drug deal, or gang violence where rival gangs are targeting each other, such as what allegedly occurred in the biker shootout in Waco, Texas.

Mass Shootings: Six Steps to Survival presents an easy-to-understand and easy-to-remember ESCAPE model for citizens of nearly any age. Equipped with this vital information, citizens will be able to learn from the actual experiences of mass shooting survivors and understand both successful and unsuccessful tactics which were utilized by these individuals. Beginning with the basics of escape and how to properly exit a public facility, through the need to conceal oneself from the offender, and finally to the last-resort effort of engagement, the average citizen will learn specific techniques to utilize in a mass shooting or violent incident.

Mass Shootings: Six Steps to Survival provides readers with the potentially life-saving information and techniques they will need to have a fighting chance in the horrifying event of a mass shooting situation.

RESEARCH

Methodology

CSI researchers utilized open-source reports including published newspaper accounts, video news reports and other Internet sources, as well as media interviews with survivors of and witnesses to mass shootings. CSI staff confirmed these accounts by using at least two sources when possible. Staff also conducted personal interviews with survivors and victims of these events.

Focus

The focus of the study was on the actions taken and decisions made by victims of mass shootings to determine if there were any patterns or commonalities which could be replicated by others facing a similar situation. Researchers were not seeking the normal "fight or flight" syndrome experienced when individuals are faced with fearful or traumatic events and involuntarily react to the situation. Rather, we specifically sought out situations where conscious actions were taken or decisions made; for example, deciding to change directions while exiting to stay away from a choke point where an attacker is focusing fire, or deciding to army-crawl along seats as opposed to standing and running.

Each mass shooting incident is unique, with its own specific set of circumstances. However, the data revealed multiple successful patterns of behavior which can be replicated by others to mitigate harm and potentially save lives.

Analysis

The case analyses which follow are drawn from nearly 80 mass shooting incidents between 1980 and 2018. This book does not purport to represent the entire text of each individual survivor's story, but simply recounts actions or tactics taken which may identify common successful techniques for survival. For each shooting incident, the primary background information is shown in the following format:

Synopsis	*General overview of the events*
Type of Establishment	*Primary place where main incident occurred*
Environment	*Indoors, outdoors or both*
Motive	*Reason for the attack, if established*
Number killed	*Number killed during a single attack or consecutive attacks by perpetrator; does not include death of perpetrator*
Number killed and injured	*Number killed and injured during a single attack or consecutive attacks by perpetrator; does not include death of perpetrator*
Date	*Date of murders*
Weapons	*Type of weapon(s) used*
Location	*City and state*
Shooter status	*Final disposition of the offender*

In 2008, the U.S. Department of Homeland Security produced a document called *Active Shooter How to Respond* and introduced its simple three-step model of *run, hide, fight*. Although well-intentioned and easy to remember, the contents of the model are debatable at best and could even be fatal if taken at face value. To the typical citizen who has little or no concept of situational awareness, "run" might mean just that – and by presenting themselves as a target to the shooter, it could make their personal situation exponentially worse. To overcome some of the fundamental shortfalls of "run, hide, fight," and to provide the public with potentially life-saving information directly from the survivors of mass shootings, the ESCAPE model (Exit, Seek Cover, Concealment, Assess, Present a Small Target, and Engage) was developed.

It is this author's hope that this book will illustrate how the ESCAPE model will provide information which may help individuals survive a deadly attack.

Case Studies - 1980s

Case #1 – First Baptist Church

Synopsis	Alvin Lee King, 45, opened fire with a rifle during a worship service at the First Baptist Church of Daingerfield.
Type of Establishment	Church
Environment	Indoors
Motive	Revenge/anger
Number killed	5
Number killed and injured	15
Date of murders	June 22, 1980
Weapons	M1 carbine with bayonet; AR-15 rifle with bayonet; .22 caliber handgun; .38 caliber handgun
Location	Daingerfield, Texas
Shooter status	Attempted suicide before being arrested. Committed suicide in prison.

Overview

Alvin Lee King had allegedly sexually molested his daughter and was scheduled to be tried for the crime on June 23, 1980. He attempted without success to find someone in the congregation of the First Baptist Church of Daingerfield to testify as a character witness on his behalf.

On the morning of June 22, King bound his wife to a kitchen chair, then dressed in combat gear and armed himself with four guns. He drove to the church and burst into the sanctuary, where the congregation was singing the offertory hymn. Shouting "This is war," King opened fire with the AR-15 rifle. In less than a minute, five people were killed and 10 were wounded.[1]

King then went across the street to a fire station and shot himself in the head. He survived the injury and was charged with murder.

ENGAGE

Witnesses went after shooter

When Red McDaniel saw that his wife had been shot, he turned toward the shooter and charged him, placing him in a bear hug. He drove King out of the church even while taking shots to the chest. McDaniel died outside the church. Kenneth Lee Truitt also went after the shooter. A witness said that when he got to the door he leaped into the air toward King, who was just outside the door. King shot him.[2]

CASE #2 – BOB MOORE'S WELDING & MACHINE SHOP	
Synopsis	Carl Robert Brown, 51, opened fire inside a welding shop and was shot dead by two witnesses as he fled the scene.
Type of Establishment	Business/workplace
Environment	Indoors
Motive	Argument/retaliation
Number killed	8
Number killed and injured	11
Date of murders	August 20, 1982
Weapon	Shotgun
Location	Miami, Florida
Shooter status	Fatally shot and run down by two witnesses, when cycling away from the crime scene.

Overview

On August 20, 1982, Navy veteran and teacher Carl Robert Brown, on psychiatric leave from his job,[3] rode his bicycle to a Miami welding and machine shop, entered through a side door, and began shooting. He was apparently angry at the $20 repair bill for work on his lawnmower engine. Brown walked through the building, methodically shooting everyone, most of the time at close range and sometimes twice, leaving three victims in the office and others in the work area and the driveway in front of the shop.[4]

Running out of ammunition, Brown stepped out of the store, reloaded and entered the shop again, to shoot twice more. He then got back on his bicycle and pedaled away. At the shop, six of the 11 employees present were dead, and two more were dying.

EXIT

Three of the injured managed to escape and jump into the car of a passing motorist, who brought them to a gas station a mile away and called for help.[5]

ENGAGE

Witnesses went after shooter

Mark Kram heard the gunshots from his nearby shop and stepped out to see what was happening. Ernest Hammett, who worked across the street, ran toward him, crying: "A bunch of people just got killed at Bob's!" Kram grabbed two guns from his office, one for himself, one for Hammett. He got behind the wheel of his car and Hammett got in the back seat. Six blocks away, he saw Brown on his bicycle.

As Kram pulled up alongside the teacher, Brown made a shoulder motion as if he were about to bring his shotgun around and open fire. Hammett, from the back seat, pointed the revolver out the driver's window. Kram said he grabbed the gun to steady Hammett's hand and fired what they meant to be a warning shot.

The bullet pierced Brown's back and severed his aorta, but Brown kept going on the bike, and “that's why I swerved my car into him," Kram said. Brown went flying into a concrete utility pole. The medical examiner’s report revealed that the gunshot killed Brown.[6]

CASE #3 – IANNI'S NIGHTCLUB	
Synopsis	Abdelkrim Belachheb, 39, opened fire at a nightclub after a woman rejected his advances.
Type of Establishment	Nightclub
Environment	Indoors
Motive	Retaliation for rejection
Number killed	6
Number killed and injured	7
Date of murders	June 29, 1984
Weapons	9mm automatic pistol
Location	Dallas, Texas
Shooter status	Sentenced to six consecutive life terms in prison in November 1984.

Overview

After a brief argument with his dance partner Marcelle Ford at upscale nightclub Ianni's, unemployed waiter Abdelkrim Belachheb, a Moroccan national allowed entry into this country despite a violent record in Europe,[7] came back into the club with a 9mm automatic pistol which he shot at Ford and four others sitting at the bar.

Belachheb went outside to reload, then came back inside and began firing again, first at the victims and then indiscriminately into the dance floor.[8] Marcelle Ford died on the way to the hospital. Belachheb later called police and admitted to the shooting and was arrested.

EXIT

Some 20 people fled the restaurant through the back door and hid behind wide pillars holding up the breezeway.[9]

CONCEALMENT

Witness Terry Rippa said he was reaching for money to pay his bar bill when he heard the gunshots. “We went under the table, and the guy went one, two, three, four, five down the row," Rippa said.[10]

ENGAGE

Ran toward shooter trying to stop him

Patron Frank Parker was in the kitchen when the shooting started. Unarmed, Parker ran out the back-kitchen door toward Belachheb. A witness stated, “Parker was coming from the back of the restaurant to the front… [he] got hit and it kind of stood him up, and then he got [shot] twice more and it dropped him…” Parker died almost immediately.[11]

Case #4 – McDonald's Restaurant

Synopsis	James Oliver Huberty, 41, opened fire in a McDonald's restaurant before he was shot dead by a police sniper.
Type of Establishment	Restaurant
Environment	Indoors and outdoors
Motive	Revenge
Number killed	21
Number killed and injured	40
Date of murders	July 18, 1984
Weapons	9mm Uzi semi-automatic; Winchester pump-action 12-gauge shotgun; 9mm Browning HP semi-automatic handgun
Location	San Ysidro, California
Shooter status	Fatally shot by SWAT team sniper the same day

Overview

James Oliver Huberty, age 41, had a history of violent behavior and domestic violence. In early 1984 the Huberty family moved from Ohio to California, where James found a job as a security guard in San Ysidro. He was dismissed from the position in early July. On July 17, Huberty called a mental health center for an appointment to try to deal with his anger but did not receive a return call.[12]

The next day he told his wife he was going to "hunt humans." Carrying an Uzi semi-automatic rifle, a shotgun, a pistol, and a bag of ammunition, he walked from his house to a McDonald's restaurant. A witness spotted Huberty carrying the firearms and called police, but the dispatcher gave officers the wrong address.[13]

Entering the restaurant, Huberty ordered those inside to lie prone and began shooting, and continued shooting for more than an hour. He fired at adults and children outside the restaurant as well. When an employee picked up the telephone to call police, the gunman began firing at those on the floor. A police officer later said that the gunman had immediately started shooting at police when they arrived.[14]

Police initially responded to a McDonald's near the U.S. border with Tijuana, and 15 minutes later learned the correct location of the shooting about two miles away. After expending more than 250 rounds of ammunition, Huberty was fatally shot by a police sniper positioned on a rooftop across the street. By the time the shooting ended, there were 21 dead and 19 wounded. The victims ranged in age from eight months to 74 years of age.[15]

EXIT/CONCEALMENT

Huberty jumped over the counter to check the kitchen and found Guillermo Flores on the floor talking to police. Also present were grill workers Alex Vasquez and Albert Leos, and three female counter workers. "Oh," Huberty observed calmly, "there's more." He cried, "You're trying to hide from me, you bastards!" and raised the Uzi. One of the women screamed in Spanish: "Don't kill me! Don't kill me!" but Huberty opened fire. The three men jumped up to flee. Flores went down a set of steps that led to an emergency exit and went outside.

Vasquez went down another stairway to an exit and escaped. Albert Leos tried to run, but one of the women grabbed him and pulled him down and he was caught in the line of fire. Wounded but still alive, he crawled to the shelter of a table, but the three female employees were dead.[16]

CONCEALMENT

When the shooting started, college student employee Ken Dickey and a co-worker fled to a basement utility room, where they were joined by three female co-workers, a woman with a baby, and a man who was bleeding. They huddled in the hot basement with gunfire sounding overhead. Finally, police knocked at the door, and though they were fearful, they opened it.[17]

OTHER
Drew gunman's attention

An 11-year-old girl lay on the restaurant floor with her eyes closed tight in fear. "I thought I heard him far away, so I opened my eyes and he saw me. He walked to the trash can and he had some [guns] in there. He got his shotgun. That's when he shot me."[18]

OTHER
Played dead

11-year-old Joshua Coleman had ridden his bicycle to McDonald's to get a soft drink. He was on the sidewalk when Joshua heard the man yell. He turned and was hit. Lying on the pavement, his right side riddled with shotgun pellets, and the gunman still shooting, Joshua played dead. How did he know to do so? "I don't know," he says. "I got lucky. . . You hear about an accident and sometimes you think, 'What would you do if you were there?' and I always thought I would play dead."[19]

ENGAGE
Confronted gunman

Huberty discharged a round into the ceiling when he entered the restaurant. Restaurant manager Neva Caine got out of her booth and went to confront the man. Huberty shot once at point-blank range and Caine died within minutes.[20]

Case #5 – U.S. Postal Service	
Synopsis	Postal worker Patrick Sherrill, 44, opened fire at a post office before committing suicide.
Type of Establishment	Workplace
Environment	Indoors
Motive	Revenge
Number killed	14
Number killed and injured	20
Date of murders	August 20, 1986
Weapons	Two .45 caliber semi-automatic pistols; .22 caliber handgun
Location	Edmond, Oklahoma
Shooter status	Committed suicide the same day by shooting himself.

Overview

Patrick Henry Sherrill was a loner whose neighbors called him "Crazy Pat" due to a long history of bizarre behavior.[21] After 16 months on the job as a permanent part-time letter carrier, he had been reprimanded by two supervisors about misdirected mail and tardy performance. Sherrill reported to a postal union steward that he was being mistreated. "I gotta get out of here," he said.[22]

At about 7:00 a.m. on August 20, Sherrill entered the post office from the employee parking lot, carrying three pistols and ammunition in a mailbag on his shoulder. Without saying a word, he gunned down one of the supervisors who had criticized him, as well as fellow postman Mike Rockne.[23]

Police arrived on scene just minutes after the shooting began. They attempted for 45 minutes to communicate with Sherrill by telephone and bullhorn, without response. When a SWAT team stormed the building at 8:30 a.m., they found the gunman's body, dead of a bullet to the head.[24] Sherrill's rampage had lasted between 15 and 20 minutes.[25]

EXIT

Sherrill chased some fleeing employees out a side exit, shooting one man, who later died in the parking lot.[26]

Employee Debbie Smith was sorting letters when the shooting began. "I froze. I couldn't run." As she hid, Sherrill passed her and opened fire on the next section. Smith ran for the front door and escaped.[27]

Richard Tompkins said, "I ran around behind some rural carrier cases trying to hide. When it got quiet I headed for the back door...the shooting started again toward the front of the post office, so I went to the back and got a door open."[28]

Peggy Gibson was nearly killed. "I hid under my case and behind the parcel tub. I ran to the back doors [found locked] ... then ran to the side door and outside."[29]

CONCEALMENT/EXIT

Darrell Fesler saw what was happening. "I heard a gunshot, and hid behind some big boxes. I looked up and saw a man shooting a gun. He shot Mike Bigler and then just turned in a circle shooting at random. He went towards the front lobby shooting and we ran out the back. He followed, still firing, and then returned inside."[30]

COVER
Hid in vault

Another employee escaped by locking herself in a vault where stamps are kept. Two other survivors hid in a broom closet.[31]

COVER
Hid in closet

Tracy Sanchez "ran to the back door, but it was locked. Another man tried to get out with me. We ran back and there was a storage closet nearby. We hid in there, but we couldn't lock it so we turned the lights off and stayed quiet. Sherrill stood by our door and kept emptying his shells and reloading his gun...Then, finally, it got quiet. But we stayed hidden until we heard the police."[32]

CONCEALMENT
Hid in open area

Sherrill bolted several doors and then systematically searched the workroom floor for workers who were cowering under tables and in cubicles. He killed three people in one work station and five in another.[33]

ENGAGE

Employee Larry Wilson tried to stop the slaughter. He said, "I kicked the gun out of Pat's hand, but he recovered it and started shooting again."[34]

OTHER
Played dead

Mike Bigler survived by playing dead. He was heading toward an exit and was shot in the back... "I just played dead. Sherrill kept walking around several times...just went around shooting methodically, saying nothing."[35]

Case #6 – Shopping Centers	
Synopsis	William Cruse, 60, killed six strangers at two shopping centers.
Type of Establishment	Shopping centers
Environment	Outdoors/indoors
Motive	Revenge/rampage
Number killed	6
Number killed and injured	20
Date of murders	April 23, 1987
Weapons	Assault rifle; shotgun; pistol
Location	Palm Bay, Florida
Shooter status	Sentenced to death on July 28, 1989; died on death row in 2009.

Overview

Just after dinner on April 23, 1987, retired librarian William Cruse charged out of his house with a shotgun to confront some teens who were bouncing a basketball in a neighbor's driveway. He fired at and wounded a 14-year-old. Then he hopped into his car and headed to the Palm Bay shopping center a half mile away. When he arrived, he started shooting. With him were at least one revolver and a .223 caliber rifle, with a satchel full of ammunition.[36]

Cruse fired toward a K Mart store, then headed toward another store, shooting a woman in a car as he drove. He opened fire in a parking lot. As Cruse was firing, police officer Ronald Grogan approached in his car; Cruse fired numerous shots into the car, killing the officer.[37] Officer Gerald Johnson arrived on scene next. Cruse shot the officer in the leg. Johnson emptied his gun at Cruse but missed. As he tried to reload, Cruse shot him and killed him.[38]

Cruse entered the Winn-Dixie store, knocked over a cash register and started firing again. As police surrounded the store, he found two women hiding in the restroom and took one of them hostage. After several hours, he let her go, after which police fired tear gas and stun grenades into the store.[39] Cruse was finally subdued and arrested.

EXIT/CONCEALMENT

Jan Roshto was in the Winn Dixie checkout line, holding her 5-month-old daughter. “It got to the back door and ran out,” she said. “Then I ran to a ditch and laid on top of my baby.”[40]

CONCEALMENT

Police found three people huddled unhurt in a refrigerated storeroom.[41]

ENGAGE

Just before he killed the officer, Cruse took aim at customer Ruben Torres. "I looked toward the glass doors, and I guess William Cruse saw me because he shot at me right through the doors and everything I had in my hand went flying," Torres recalled. "After that I crawled up to the window and saw him walking across the parking lot. I don't know where I got the strength from, but I took the doors off the track and got out of the store.” [42]

As Cruse killed Officer Johnson, Torres ran to his car and “I got my gun out of my glove compartment and we started a little shootout,” he said. "I was shooting at him and he was shooting at me." When Torres went back to his car for more ammunition, a police officer stopped him, thinking he was a second gunman. Torres was later credited with distracting Cruse, allowing people to escape from the grocery store. [43]

OTHER

Hostage response

Robin Brown, 21, held hostage for six hours, communicated with the shooter. She says she wiped blood from the gunman’s hands, helped him smash store lights, and fed him potato chips. "I tried to get him to surrender. I stopped him from killing himself and from killing me.”[44]

Case #7 – Electromagnetic Systems Lab	
Synopsis	Silicon Valley defense plant employee Richard Wade Farley, 39, shot and killed seven and wounded four more at his company's office.
Type of Establishment	Workplace
Environment	Indoors and outdoors
Motive	Revenge after being spurned
Number killed	7
Number killed and injured	11
Date of murders	February 16, 1988
Weapons	Benelli semi-automatic shotgun; pump-action shotgun; rifle; four handguns
Location	Sunnyvale, California
Shooter status	In December 1991, sentenced to death in gas chamber; ruling upheld in July 2009.[45]

Overview

At Electromagnetic Systems Lab (ESL), Richard Wade Farley was obsessed with co-worker Laura Black and had stalked her for several years. In the autumn of 1985 the Human Resources department of the company ordered Farley to attended counseling sessions which he did, but he continued the harassment of Black. By the following spring, Farley was threatening fellow employees. That along with his poor work performance resulted in his termination in May of 1986. Even after his employment at another company, he continued his stalking. Black was granted a temporary restraining order against Farley, and he was ordered to leave her alone pending a full hearing on February 17, 1988.[46]

On February 16, Farley drove to the ESL parking lot with a "Benelli semi-automatic shotgun, a rifle with a scope, a pump-action shotgun, a Sentinel revolver, a Smith & Wesson .357 Magnum revolver, a Browning semi-automatic pistol, a Smith & Wesson pistol, a smoke bomb, a belt with pouches filled with ammunition, other bags containing more than 200 rounds of ammunition, and a vest containing more than 800 rounds of ammunition...a foot-long buck knife and sheath, and ear protectors."[47] He walked into a side door by shooting the glass, and continued shooting as he headed to Black's second-floor office. When he reached the office she slammed the door, but he fired through the door. The first shot missed but the second hit her in the shoulder, and she fell to the floor unconscious.

Farley held a police SWAT team at bay for five hours, speaking on the telephone numerous times with the hostage negotiator. He eventually surrendered to police. He had expended 98 rounds of ammunition.[48] Seven people lay dead, and four more were wounded.

In October of 1991 Farley was convicted of seven counts of first-degree murder, and later sentenced to death.

CONCEALMENT/EXIT

Lisa Black was shot, and she and other survivors hid from Farley while he was holding the SWAT team at bay. They later escaped.[49]

OTHER

Released by gunman

Linda Walden, the shooter's friend and former landlady, was hiding under the desk at which Farley was standing while he was on the telephone with police. He pulled out the desk chair and saw her and said, "Oh, there's someone here. You can come out now. Oh, it's Linda." When she emerged, Farley told her she could leave. Employee Christine Hansen, hiding nearby, thought the police were evacuating the building and she came out of hiding. When she saw Farley, she asked if she could leave, too, and he told her, "Yes, you can go."[50]

Case #8 – Cleveland Elementary School

Synopsis	Patrick Purdy, 26, opened fire at Cleveland Elementary School, and then committed suicide.
Type of Establishment	School
Environment	Outdoors
Motive	Racial
Number killed	5
Number killed and injured	35
Date of murders	January 17, 1989
Weapons	AK-47-type semi-automatic assault rifle; two handguns
Location	Stockton, California
Shooter status	Committed suicide the same day by shooting himself in the head.

Overview

On January 17, 1989, at 11.40 a.m., former Stockton resident Patrick Purdy, a disturbed loner with guerrilla-warfare fantasies,[51] parked his car outside the Cleveland Elementary School, got out, set it alight by means of a gasoline-filled beer bottle, and walked toward the school. Some 300 pupils were outside at recess.

Purdy was dressed in battle gear and wearing a flak jacket. He entered the school grounds through a gap in the fence, carrying two handguns and an AK-47. He opened fire at a group of portable classrooms, then moved away and fired across the blacktop where children were playing, toward the main building about 250 yards away. Several rounds went completely through the main school building and came out the other side.[52]

When the four-minute assault ended, five young children were dead; one teacher and 29 pupils were wounded.[53] The dead were all Southeast Asians from war-refugee groups which comprised more than 70% of the school's enrollment. A report to the California

Attorney General indicated that Purdy blamed all minorities for his failings, and "selected Southeast Asians because they were the minority with whom he was most in contact."[54]

ASSESS

Teacher Lori Mackey said she ran to her classroom window when she heard what she thought were firecrackers. When she realized what was happening, she took her 10 pupils into a rear room where they could not be seen.[55]

Case #9 – Standard Gravure Printing Co.	
Synopsis	Joseph T. Wesbecker, 47, gunned down eight people at his former workplace before committing suicide.
Type of Establishment	Workplace
Environment	Indoors
Motive	Revenge
Number killed	8
Number killed and injured	20
Date of murders	September 14, 1989
Weapons	AK-47 semi-automatic rifle; two MAC-11 semi-automatic pistols; .38 caliber revolver; 9mm automatic pistol; bayonet
Location	Louisville, Kentucky
Shooter status	Committed suicide the same day by shooting himself.

Overview

Joseph Wesbecker had worked for printing company Standard Gravure for 17 years but went on disability leave in the spring of 1989 because of mental illness. He had a history of suicide attempts.

On September 14, 1989 at about 8:30 a.m., Wesbecker entered the Standard Gravure plant carrying a duffel bag containing an AK-47 semi-automatic rifle, two MAC-11 semi-automatic pistols, a .38-caliber revolver, a 9mm automatic pistol, and a bayonet, along with thousands of rounds of ammunition.[56] He took the elevator to the executive reception area and, as soon as the doors opened, fired at receptionists Sharon Needy, killing her, and Angela Bowman, leaving her paralyzed by a shot in the back. Searching for Michael Shea (president of Standard Gravure) and other supervisors and bosses, Wesbecker calmly walked through the hallways, deliberately shooting at people.[57] Wesbecker eventually went to the pressroom, put a gun under his chin, and killed himself. He had killed eight people and wounded 12.

EXIT/COVER

Employee John Tingle encountered Wesbecker at the beginning of the rampage. Wesbecker said to him, “I told them I’d be back. Get out of my way, John.” “{Tingle} said, ‘How are you, Rock?’” He said, “Fine, John. Back off and get out of my way.” Tingle and other nearby employees fled to a restroom and locked the door.[58]

Case Studies - 1990s

Case #10 – General Motors Acceptance Corp.

Synopsis	James Edward Pough, 42, opened fire at an auto loan company office before committing suicide.
Type of Establishment	Business
Environment	Indoors
Motive	Revenge
Number killed	9
Number killed and injured	13
Date of murders	June 18, 1990
Weapons	.30 caliber M1 assault rifle; .38 revolver (9mm semi-automatic left in car)
Location	Jacksonville, Florida
Shooter status	Committed suicide the same day by shooting himself.

Overview

James Edward Pough's car had been repossessed by General Motors Acceptance Corporation in January of 1990, and he later received a bill for more than $6,000 in outstanding charges.[59] Besides his financial problems, his marriage had apparently broken up that month, and his wife had obtained a protective order to keep him away from her for a year.[60]

On June 17 Pough killed a pimp and a prostitute who were standing on a corner not far from his home in Jacksonville. About ten minutes after those murders Pough shot and wounded two youths, 17 and 18 years of age, after asking them for directions.[61]

The next morning, Pough drove to the GMAC office. Leaving a 9mm semi-automatic pistol in the trunk of his Buick, he entered the building through the front door, and without saying a word, immediately began shooting with an M1 carbine, killing customer Julia Burgess at the front counter.[62]

David Hendricks, 26, was standing at the counter making a payment when he heard a worker scream. At that instant, he was shot in the back. As he turned, Pough fired three more shots into him.[63]

As Pough walked through the office, he moved from desk to desk, shooting at employees hiding underneath.[64] He then shot and killed himself. Eight employees were dead and 12 were wounded.

EXIT

When the GMAC employees realized what was happening, many of them were able to escape through a back door of the building.[65]

CONCEALMENT

When someone hollered "Get down!" some in the office realized what was happening and dived under desks and were trapped there. Pough began picking off persons who were ducking for cover and shot at least eight people one by one. All those killed were shot two to four times, mostly as they crouched under their desks in an attempt to hide.[66]

CASE #11 – LUBY'S CAFETERIA	
Synopsis	George Hennard, 35, drove his pickup into a cafeteria and opened fire on those inside before committing suicide.
Type of Establishment	Business
Environment	Indoors
Motive	Revenge
Number killed	23
Number killed and injured	43[i]
Date of murders	October 16, 1991
Weapons	Glock 17 pistol; Ruger P89 pistol
Location	Killeen, Texas
Shooter status	Committed suicide by shooting himself in the head after being cornered and wounded by police.

Overview

George Hennard, the son of a retired Army officer, lived with his mother in Belton, Texas, not far from Killeen where Fort Hood is located. He received an honorable discharge after serving two years in the Navy and then joined the Merchant Marine in 1977. He was discharged in 1989 under less than honorable conditions, having been found twice with drugs and becoming more combative with shipmates.

In February 1991, Hennard learned that his attempt to return to seagoing status had been denied. Despite having a history of drug abuse, he purchased two pistols and ammunition.[67]

On October 16 at 12:39 p.m., Hennard drove his pickup truck through the front window of the Luby's Cafeteria in Killeen and, armed

[i] At least 20 people were injured by Hennard's vehicle or from being shot; others were injured by flying glass or from fleeing the scene.

with two semi-automatic pistols, began firing at those inside. Several of the diners thought the crash was accidental and went to help the driver, only to be shot down.

Hennard shouted, "This is what Bell County has done to me!" As he continued shooting, often at point-blank range into the victim's head, he yelled, "Is it worth it? Tell me, is it worth it?"[68] He repeatedly emptied and reloaded his pistols, methodically killing the diners.[69]

By the time police arrived, Hennard had killed 22 (one died later) and wounded 20. He exchanged gunfire with officers for a few minutes, then ran toward the restrooms and shot himself in the head. The entire incident had lasted only about 10 minutes.[70]

Hennard's former roommate told a reporter that he was not surprised by the murders. He said that Hennard had talked about killing himself, saying that he didn't have any friends or girlfriends, and that he didn't respect his mother.[71]

EXIT

Hazel Holley, age 71, broke her arm as she escaped through a broken window.[72] The gunman faced down another patron, Sam Wink, but when a woman nearby tried to run away he was distracted and fired at her, which allowed Wink to flee.[73]

EXIT
Helped others

Customer Tommy Vaughn, 6'6" and 300 lbs. in weight, threw himself through the front window and broke it, allowing 20 to 30 people to escape.[74]

COVER

One woman survived by hiding in a freezer; she was later treated for hypothermia.[75] Food preparer Mark Matthews, age 19, escaped by hiding inside an industrial dishwasher. He was so frightened that he did not come out until the following day.[76]

CONCEALMENT

The attack was so sudden and terrifying that patrons and restaurant workers could only duck under tables, chairs and benches, clasping hands and praying.[77]

OTHER

Gunman allowed two to leave

The gunman allowed a mother and her four-year-old child to leave. In his only show of mercy, he pointed a pistol at a blood-splattered Anica McNeil, who'd just seen her mother shot dead and said, "You with the baby—get out."[78]

Case #12 – University of Iowa	
Synopsis	Former graduate student Gang Lu, 28, went on a rampage on campus and then committed suicide.
Type of Establishment	School/university
Environment	Indoors
Motive	Revenge
Number killed	5
Number killed and injured	6
Date of murders	November 1, 1991
Weapons	.38 caliber revolver; .22 caliber handgun
Location	Iowa City, Iowa
Shooter status	Committed suicide the same day by shooting himself.

Overview

Gang Lu, born in Beijing, China, was a graduate student in physics at the University of Iowa who had received his doctoral degree from that university the previous May. Gang was upset that his dissertation was not awarded a prestigious dissertation prize which included a monetary award, which was instead awarded to another student.[79]

On November 1, 1991, at about 3:40 in the afternoon, Gang attended a physics and astronomy department meeting. Shortly after the meeting began, he pulled a revolver from his jacket and began shooting. He killed the department chair and two professors (all of whom had been involved in Gang's doctoral work), and then shot and killed rival Linhua Shan, the prize winner.[80]

Gang left the building, crossed two streets, entered another building and went to the second floor. He shot and killed the associate vice president for academic affairs (whose office had denied the dissertation prize) and shot and wounded a student working in the office.[81]

Entering an empty conference room, Gang took off his jacket, folded it, and then killed himself, 12 minutes after he had fired the first shot.[82]

CONCEALMENT

As students scrambled to find cover, one crawled under a table but was shot in the hand and chest.[83]

Case #13 – Lindhurst High school	
Synopsis	Former student Eric Houston, 20, killed three students and a teacher and wounded 10 others at Lindhurst High School before surrendering to police after an eight-hour standoff.
Type of Establishment	School
Environment	Indoors
Motive	Revenge
Number killed	4
Number killed and injured	14
Date of murders	May 1, 1992
Weapons	12-gauge pump-action shotgun; sawed-off .22 caliber rifle
Location	Olivehurst, California
Shooter status	Sentenced to death in September 1993; sentence upheld by California Supreme Court in 2012.[84]

Overview

20-year-old Eric Houston, a former student at Lindhurst High School, had not graduated from the school due to a failing grade from his Civics teacher.[85] On May 1, 1992, at just before 3:00 p.m., Houston came to the school campus armed with a 12-gauge pump-action shotgun and a sawed off .22 caliber rifle, wearing military camouflage with bandoliers across his chest.[86] As he entered the school, he fatally shot teacher Robert Brens, who had been Houston's Civics teacher his senior year. He then shot and killed Judy Davis, a student who was inside Brens' classroom.[87]

Houston then walked through the hallway outside the classroom and fatally shot student Jason Edward White in the chest. Houston pointed his shotgun at a female student, but before he could fire his weapon, student Beamon Hill pushed her aside and took the shotgun blast to the side of his head.[88]

Houston then entered a classroom with about 25 to 30 students inside. He sent a student to retrieve more hostages, and eventually held more than 80 students hostage. After negotiations with police, he released some of the hostages. He surrendered to police after an eight-hour standoff.[89]

CONCEALMENT

Johnny Mills recalled that "our teacher…poked his head out the door to see what the ruckus was and immediately slammed the door shut and yelled, 'Get down! Get down!' Now we all looked at him in shock and he said, 'They are shooting! Get down!' I dove to the ground and crawled to the back of the right stage and huddled in the corner."[90]

Sophomore Jennifer Thompson said she heard shots in bursts. "Bang, bang, bang. Silence, then again," she said, adding that her teacher first thought it was firecrackers. Then students slid under their desks as they had been trained to do.[91]

Case #14 – Law Firm Office Building	
Synopsis	Gian Luigi Ferri, 55, opened fire throughout an office building before committing suicide inside as police pursued him.
Type of Establishment	Business
Environment	Indoors
Motive	Uncertain; suspected revenge
Number killed	8
Number killed and injured	14
Date of murders	July 1, 1993
Weapons	Two TEC-9 semi-automatic handguns; .45 semi-automatic pistol
Location	San Francisco, California
Shooter status	Committed suicide the same day by shooting himself.

Overview

Gian Luigi Ferri was apparently dissatisfied with the legal services he had received from the law firm of Pettit & Martin. At just before 3:00 p.m. on July 1, 1993, he entered the firm's office building and made his way to the 34th floor where the firm's office was located. Exiting the elevator, Ferri opened fire with a pair of TEC-9 handguns and a .45 pistol. After roaming the floor, he took the stairs down one flight and continued shooting. Eight people were killed in the attack and six others were injured.[92]

EXIT/CONCEALMENT

The gunman fired through the conference room's glass window, killing two people on the spot. One woman hid under a table, and another ran for her life, while being shot five times.[93]

Down the hall, John Scully heard the shooting and ran down a staircase to an empty office on the 33rd floor where his wife was. They ran toward the elevator to escape but were confronted by the gunman. As Ferri aimed, Scully put himself in front of his wife and was fatally wounded.[94]

ENGAGE/EXIT/CONCEALMENT

Verbally engaged with gunman

Survivor Charles Ross said that "The gunman was cold, detached, impassive, as if I could be anybody. It made me realize that I had to be as cold-blooded to him as he was to me." Ross slammed his door shut, but Ferri opened it. Ross yelled "Who the hell are you?" and pushed past the gunman and ran down two corridors, then ducked into a room to hide.[95]

CASE #15 – LUIGI'S RESTAURANT

Synopsis	Army Sgt. Kenneth Junior French, 22, opened fire inside an Italian restaurant while ranting about gays in the military, before he was shot and arrested by police.
Type of Establishment	Restaurant
Environment	Indoors
Motive	Unknown
Number killed	4
Number killed and injured	12
Date of murders	August 6, 1993
Weapons	Pump shotgun
Location	Fayetteville, North Carolina
Shooter status	In 1994, sentenced to four consecutive life terms plus 35 years.

Overview

On the night of August 6, 1993, Kenneth Junior French got out of a truck near Luigi's Restaurant and a Kroger supermarket in Fayetteville, North Carolina. Wearing a hunting vest and carrying a pump shotgun, he began firing toward the Kroger store. He then walked to the back of the restaurant and entered through the kitchen area. Hollering "freeze," French walked through the restaurant and killed four people and wounded others, often firing right in people's faces after they asked for mercy.[96]

Witnesses reported that during the shootings, French shouted, "I'll show you, Clinton, about letting gays into the army."[97] French claimed that before the rampage, he had consumed about a fifth of whiskey while watching the movie "The Unforgiven," which includes a scene of a violent massacre at a saloon.[98]

A Fayetteville police officer was working off-duty at Kroger and heard the shots. He called for backup, entered Luigi's, and shot

French. As another officer approach French raised his gun; the second officer fired twice. The shotgun was taken from French and he was arrested and taken to a hospital for surgery. Four people were dead and eight more were wounded.

EXIT/CONCEALMENT

As the shooting began, restaurant patrons began running out the door and hiding under tables.[99]

CONCEALMENT

Protected loved ones

Restaurant patron James Kidd hid in a booth and covered his son. The gunman shot Kidd, who died almost immediately. The son was not physically harmed.[100]

ASSESS/ENGAGE

Drew attention of the shooter

Restaurant cook Willie McCormick was the first person shot when he tried to walk away from the gunman, but he survived.

Restaurant proprietor Pete Parrous approached French and asked him not to hurt anyone. Parrous was shot in the face and died instantly. As he fell, his wife stood up screaming and French shot her. Mrs. Parrous fell beside her daughter, who began screaming and who was shot in the thigh.

Wesley Cover had been tending to a patron who had been hit by a pellet from the shooting. He asked the gunman not to hurt the woman he was helping because she was pregnant. Mr. Cover was then shot in the head and died. The woman was also shot, but not fatally.[101]

CASE #16 – LONG ISLAND RAILROAD	
Synopsis	Colin Ferguson, 35, opened fire on a commuter train from New York City's Pennsylvania Station. He was tackled by three passengers when he stopped to reload.
Type of Establishment	Commuter train
Environment	Indoors
Motive	Racial
Number killed	6
Number killed and injured	25
Date of murders	December 7, 1993
Weapons	Ruger P89 9mm semi-automatic pistol
Location	Long Island, New York
Shooter status	Sentenced to six consecutive 25-years-to-life terms on February 17, 1995.

Overview

On December 7, 1993, Colin Ferguson purchased a ticket at Pennsylvania Station in New York City and boarded the third car of the eastbound Long Island Railroad 5:33 evening commuter train to Hicksville, along with 80 other passengers. Ferguson sat at one end of the car, carrying a handgun and a canvas bag filled with 160 rounds of ammunition.[102]

As the train approached the Merillon Avenue Station, Ferguson drew the gun, dropped several cartridges on the ground, stood up and started opening fire on the passengers at random, but apparently targeting white people.[103] He was finally tackled and held by passengers until he could be arrested.

Colin defended himself at his trial, claiming that he was the victim of a racist conspiracy.[104] In February 1995 he was convicted and sentenced to six consecutive 25-years-to-life sentences.

EXIT

The train's engineer learned of the shooting, but he decided against opening the train doors because two of the cars were not yet at the platform. Although an announcement was made ordering conductors not to open the doors, one conductor climbed out of a train window and opened a door of the third car from the outside so that passengers could escape.[105]

EXIT/CONCEALMENT

Ferguson walked east on the train, pulling the trigger steadily about every half second. Some passengers tried to hide underneath the seats; others ran to the eastern end of the train and tried to go into the next car. [106]

CONCEALMENT

At the front of the car, William Warshowsky was waiting by the door as the train approached the station when he heard the pop of the 9-millimeter gunfire and mistook it for caps or fireworks. "A woman yelled, 'He's got a gun! He's shooting people!'" the passenger recalled. He jumped down into a seat to hide as the bullets sprayed the car.[107]

ENGAGE

Ferguson emptied two 15-round magazines during the shooting. As he was reloading a third magazine, passengers Michael O'Connor, Kevin Blum and Mark McEntee tackled the gunman and pinned him to one of the train's seats. Other passengers ran to grab his arms and legs and help hold him down. Andrew Roderick, an off-duty Long Island Rail Road policeman, boarded the train car and handcuffed Ferguson.[108]

OTHER

Played dead

Gunshot victim Mary Anne Phillips testified that she had played dead after being wounded. She said she kept her eyes closed so that Ferguson would not come back and shoot her again.[109]

Case #17 – Chuck E. Cheese Restaurant

Synopsis	Nathan Dunlap, 33, went on a rampage through his former workplace and was arrested the following day.
Type of Establishment	Restaurant
Environment	Indoors
Motive	Revenge/robbery
Number killed	4
Number killed and injured	5
Date of murders	December 14, 1993
Weapons	Small caliber semi-automatic handgun
Location	Aurora, Colorado
Shooter status	Sentenced to death on May 17, 1996. In February 2013 the U.S. Supreme Court declined to hear his appeal,[110] and in October 2014 his execution was indefinitely postponed by Colorado Gov. John Hickenlooper.

Overview

On the night of December 14, 1993, Nathan Dunlap entered the Chuck E Cheese restaurant from which he had recently been dismissed as a kitchen worker. He ordered a sandwich, played a video game, and then hid in the restroom until closing. When employees were cleaning up, he confronted and shot two workers, shot a third one in a hallway, shot and wounded another in the kitchen, before robbing and killing the manager in her office.[111] Then he grabbed her bag, filled it with game tokens, key chains, cards, $1,591 and change, and shot her again.

Employee Sylvia Crowell was cleaning the salad bar when Dunlap came up behind her. He raised his pistol to her left ear and pulled the trigger. Employee Ben Grant, a high school junior, was vacuuming. Dunlap shot him in the face and killed him.[112]

The shooting spree lasted only about five minutes. Dunlap was arrested about 12 hours after the murders.[113]

EXIT

After being shot, Bobby Stevens fled the restaurant and ran to nearby apartments to call the police.[114]

OTHER

Pleaded for life

Colleen O'Connor saw Dunlap coming and knelt in front of him to beg for her life. As she raised her arms, he held a gun just 18 inches from her head. "Don't shoot," she cried. "I won't tell." "I have to," the shooter said as he pulled the trigger.[115]

CASE #18 – FAIRCHILD AIR FORCE BASE

Synopsis	Former airman Dean Allen Mellberg, 20, opened fire inside a hospital at the Fairchild Air Force Base before he was shot dead by a military police officer.
Type of Establishment	Air Force Base hospital
Environment	Indoors
Motive	Revenge
Number killed	4
Number killed and injured	26
Date of murders	June 20, 1994
Weapons	Chinese-made MAK-90 assault rifle
Location	Spokane County, Washington
Shooter status	Shot and killed by military police officer.

Overview

Dean A. Mellberg had been discharged from the U.S. Air Force for chronic problems. Major Thomas E. Brigham, psychiatrist, and Captain Alan W. London, psychologist, had both recommended his discharge. On June 21, 1994, Mellberg entered the Fairchild Air Force Base hospital annex carrying a duffel bag containing a Chinese-made MAK-90 assault rifle. He went to a restroom inside the annex, where he removed the rifle from the duffel bag. He then went to the office shared by Major Brigham and Captain London and killed them both with two bursts of gunfire.[116]

Mellberg proceeded down the corridors of the annex and sprayed them with round after round as panic-stricken patients and medical personnel ran for their lives. He then entered the adjoining main hospital building and began shooting in the cafeteria.[117]

After several minutes inside the annex and the main building, Mr. Mellberg left and went to the parking lot, where he killed Anita Linder, the 62-year-old wife of a retired serviceman.

Senior Airman Andrew Brown with the security police was patrolling on a bicycle when he received an emergency call on his radio. He rode a quarter-mile to the scene, and spotted Mellberg shooting in the parking lot. Brown ordered the gunman to drop his weapon; Mellberg turned and shot at the officer. Brown returned fire, killing the gunman with two shots to the head.[118]

OTHER

Gunman's choice

As Mellberg burst through the door of the office shared by Maj. Brigham and Capt. London, Tiffany Williams was just finishing her therapy session with Capt. London. Mellberg shot London in the chest. He aimed the rifle at Williams, they locked eyes, and then Mellberg turned and left. Williams immediately called 911 and reported the shooting.[119]

Case #19 – Walter Rossler Co.	
Synopsis	Former metallurgist James Daniel Simpson, 28, opened fire throughout the company where he had worked, killing five before committing suicide.
Type of Establishment	Business
Environment	Indoors
Motive	Unknown (mental illness)
Number killed	5
Number killed and injured	5
Date of murders	April 3, 1995
Weapons	Ruger 9mm pistol; .32 revolver
Location	Corpus Christi, Texas
Shooter status	Committed suicide the same day by shooting himself.

Overview

28-year-old James Simpson had worked for a year as a metallurgist at the Walter Rossler Co., a refinery inspection company in Corpus Christi, Texas, before quitting in September 1994.

On April 3, 1995, he walked into the company through the front door, carrying a 9mm semi-automatic pistol and a .32 caliber revolver. He walked up to employee Wendy Gilmore, said, "This is for you, bitch," and shot her. He then shot owner Walter Rossler, Rossler's wife Joan, and two other employees. The gunman then walked out the back door and shot himself behind the building as police closed in.[120]

According to police, the motive for the shooting was Simpson's apparent depression.[121]

EXIT

As Simpson shot Wendy Gilmore, Joan Rossler and the other secretary ran. Rossler was shot and killed.[122]

CONCEALMENT

Lisa Rossler-Duff, daughter of the company's owners, grabbed her 8-month-old-son and crawled under a desk, then ran to another office and called 911.[123]

Case #20 – Freddie's Fashion Mart	
Synopsis	Roland J. Smith, 51, opened fire inside a Harlem clothing store, also setting it on fire, then committed suicide.
Type of Establishment	Business
Environment	Indoors
Motive	Racial
Number killed	7
Number killed and injured	11
Date of murders	December 8, 1995
Weapons	Gun (and fire causing death by smoke inhalation)
Location	Harlem, New York City, New York
Shooter status	Committed suicide the same day by shooting himself.

Overview

Freddie's Fashion Mart, a Jewish-owned business located across the street from the famous Apollo Theater, had been picketed for weeks in a dispute over the rent raise to the black-owned sub-tenant Record Shack. The picketers claimed that Freddie's did not employ blacks and was behind the threatened eviction of the Record Shack.[124]

On December 8, at 10:12 a.m., Roland James Smith, Jr., a Harlem resident with a criminal record going back 30 years who had been among the picketers, walked into Freddie's, pulled out a gun, shouted for people to get out, kicked over a table, spilled paint thinner on several bins of clothing and set them on fire, and began shooting.[125]

After exchanging gunfire with police, Smith set several fires in the store. The intensity of the fire prevented police and firefighters from gaining access inside the store for more than two hours. They found three bodies huddled together in a back room on the first floor and four more in the basement. Seven of the victims apparently died of smoke inhalation.[126] Smith was found dead inside with a gun in his hand.

EXIT

Four wounded people managed to stumble out of the store before the fire enveloped it.[127]

Case #21 – Municipal Office

Synopsis	Fired city park employee Clifton McCree, 41, opened fire on former coworkers inside their municipal trailer, then committed suicide.
Type of Establishment	Government office
Environment	Indoors
Motive	Revenge/racial
Number killed	5
Number killed and injured	6
Date of murders	February 9, 1996
Weapon	Glock 9mm semi-automatic pistol
Location	Fort Lauderdale, Florida
Shooter status	Committed suicide the same day by shooting himself.

Overview

Clifton McCree had worked for the city of Fort Lauderdale park department for 18 years. He was fired for rudeness to the public, threatening co-workers, and failing a drug test. He threatened to return to his workplace and "do things."[128]

Fourteen months later, at 5:00 a.m. on February 9, 1996, McCree went to a temporary trailer office a block from the beach and systematically began firing on the beach cleaning crew he once worked with as they sat around a table preparing for work. Armed with a 9mm semi-automatic handgun, he burst through the door and said, "Everyone's going to die," then pulled out the pistol and began shooting, killing five co-workers and critically wounding another. He then turned the gun on himself and committed suicide. A suicide note he left behind stated that the shootings were "to punish some of the cowardly, racist devils" that got him fired.[129]

EXIT

When McCree burst through the door, he cried, "Everyone's going to die," and pulled out a pistol. The workers ran for the exits. McCree fired 10 shots, inserted another magazine, and fired again.[130]

OTHER

Played dead

The first to be wounded, Lelan Brookins, survived the massacre by playing dead.[131]

Case #22 – R. E. Phelon Co. Plant	
Synopsis	Hastings Arthur Wise, 43, opened fire at the R.E. Phelon Company in retaliation for being fired after an argument with a supervisor.
Type of Establishment	Workplace/business
Environment	Indoors/outdoors
Motive	Revenge
Number killed	4
Number killed and injured	7
Date of murders	September 15, 1997
Weapon	9mm pistol
Location	Aiken, South Carolina
Shooter status	Executed by lethal injection in South Carolina on November 4, 2005.

Overview

Hastings Arthur Wise was a 6’4” 4 ex-con who weighed more than 250 pounds. Although he had spent almost 15 years cleaning up his life, he seemed to enjoy intimidating co-workers by talking about his time in prison for breaking into a house and robbing a bank. After four years working at the Phelon lawnmower ignition plant, he was fired after a violent confrontation with a supervisor.[132]

Weeks later, Wise returned to the plant. He waited for the afternoon shift change when those who he thought had led to his firing, or who had gotten jobs he wanted were there.[133] Security guard Stanley Vance saw Wise pull up in his car. Wise shot Vance in the chest, then yanked out the phone lines in the guard shack and told the guard "I got things to do."[134]

Witnesses testified that Wise entered through a side door, went directly to the personnel office, and shot 56-year-old Charles Griffeth twice in the back. Griffeth had fired Wise two months earlier.[135]

Wise began firing his pistol at everyone around, killing David Moore and Leonard Filyaw and wounding two others.

Panicked workers were running to escape. Wise next found Sheryl Wood, who got a quality control job he had wanted. He shot her in the back and leg, and then put a bullet in her head. After that, he fired several more shots, but no one else was killed.

Wise attempted suicide in the plant by drinking insecticide but failed.[136] He was taken into custody by SWAT officers.

EXIT

Eyewitnesses said they ran from the plant as other workers and supervisors came through shouting, "There's a man with a gun." People were running as fast as they could, yelling “Get out! Get out!”[137]

Worker John Goad said, "I could hear the shots, and I could hear people screaming," he said. “I knew I had to go...So I ran out the way I came"[138]

CONCEALMENT

Two men and a woman hid under desks on the first floor, communicating with a 911 dispatcher by portable telephone.[139]

OTHER

Gunman had specific targets

Wise shoved employee Carol Woody aside as he went into the Human Resources office doorway. Pam Holley was on the telephone at her desk in the outer office when Wise rushed in, searching for Charles Griffeth. The killer passed up dozens of employees during his rampage, including Zach Bush. The two looked at each other before Wise went to another area of the plant. At his trial, Wise said he didn't shoot Bush because the two had gotten along.[140]

OTHER

Pleaded for life

When Wise returned to the outer office he found Pam Morey. "He put the gun between my eyes," she said. He then ordered her off the phone and yanked it out of the wall. "I just started pleading and praying. I said, 'I have kids. I'm a single mother. Please don't kill me,'" Mrs. Holley said. Distracted by someone who entered the building, Wise left the room. Terrified, Morey hid under her desk "because I didn't want to see somebody get shot." When she eventually heard shots farther off, she jumped up and ran from the building.[141]

Case #23 – Caltrans Maintenance Yard	
Synopsis	Former Caltrans employee Arturo Reyes Torres, 41, opened fire at maintenance yard after being fired.
Type of Establishment	Workplace
Environment	Outdoors
Motive	Revenge
Number killed	4
Number killed and injured	6
Date of murders	December 19, 1997
Weapons	AK-47-type semi-automatic assault rifle; shotgun; handgun
Location	Orange, California
Shooter status	Shot and killed by police in a gun battle the same day.

Overview

Arturo Torres, a former Marine, had worked for Caltrans in Orange County, California for 12 years. In mid-1997 he took $106.50 worth of highway scrap metal after being warned by a supervisor that it was against the rules. Torres was fired from his job, and unsuccessfully appealed the firing to state authorities.[142]

On December 19, 1997, Torres drove his car through the front gate of the Caltrans maintenance yard, walked out into the rain, and started firing with an AK-47 assault rifle.[143] Torres was also armed with a shotgun and a handgun.

He first went for the supervisor whom he believed unfairly targeted him for dismissal. Then he walked around a suite of trailer offices and fired, fatally wounding three men inside. The gunman had a clear view through the windows of workers as they scrambled for cover. According to police, more than 300 bullets were fired in all.[144]

Police exchanged gunfire with Reyes and chased him to a nearby intersection. Torres jumped out of his car and pulled his weapon on the driver of another car. He fired, but the driver ducked and was not hit. As the shooter went back toward his car, a gunfight with police erupted, leaving Torres dead and an officer wounded.[145]

CONCEALMENT

One employee called 911 as he hid under his desk. "Help, help, there's gunfire everywhere."[146]

Case #24 – Connecticut State Lottery Headquarters

Synopsis	Lottery worker Matthew Beck, 35, gunned down four bosses before committing suicide.
Type of Establishment	Workplace (state government facility)
Environment	Indoors to outdoors
Motive	Revenge
Number killed	4
Number killed and injured	4
Date of murders	March 6, 1998
Weapon	Glock semi-automatic pistol
Location	Newington, Connecticut
Shooter status	Committed suicide the same day by shooting himself.

Overview

In October of 1997, Matthew Beck, an eight-year-employee at the Connecticut State Lottery, had been granted a leave of absence for stress-related problems and was undergoing medical treatment. He had been upset about being required to perform duties that were not in his job description. When he returned to work in February, he was waiting to see if he would receive back pay. During his medical absence, a higher-paying position had been filled and he was upset that he had not received it.[147]

On March 6, 1998, Beck came to work armed with a Glock semi-automatic handgun, a butcher knife, and three magazines containing at least 19 rounds each. Half an hour after reporting to work, he left his office and headed for the executive suites, where he pulled out his weapons and started shooting supervisors.[148]

Beck walked first into the office of information services chief Michael Logan. He shot Logan and stabbed him with the butcher knife. He then shot chief financial officer Linda Mlynarczyk and Rick Rubelmann, vice president of operations. Beck pointed his gun at Mlynarczyk and said, "Bye, bye," and shot her three times.[149] He also killed Rubelmann. He then chased lottery chief Otho Brown into a parking lot and shot him.

As two detectives approached Beck, he put the gun to his temple and shot himself. He died a few hours later.[150]

EXIT

The sound of gunshots sent terrified workers running for the doors, where a security guard yelled for them to run for the woods nearby.[151]

EXIT/OTHER

Pleaded for life

Lottery president Otho Brown ran from the building with Beck in pursuit. Brown stumbled in the parking lot, apparently after losing a shoe.[152] He fell to ground, raised his hands, and begged, "Don't kill me, don't kill me." Beck replied, "Aw, shut up," and shot him.[153]

COVER

About 20 workers took refuge in another part of the building used by a paint distributor.[154]

Case #25 – Westside Middle School

Synopsis	Mitchell Scott Johnson, 13, and Andrew Douglas Golden, 11, ambushed students and teachers as they left their middle school in response to a fire alarm.
Type of Establishment	School
Environment	Outdoors
Motive	Unknown
Number killed	5
Number killed and injured	15
Date of murders	March 24, 1998
Weapons	M1 carbine .30 caliber replica carbine; .38 caliber derringer; .22 caliber derringer; two .38 caliber revolvers; two .380 caliber pistols; .357 caliber revolver; .44 magnum rifle; Remington 742 30.06 caliber rifle[155]
Location	Jonesboro, Arkansas
Shooter status	Sentenced to confinement until age 21. Johnson was released on August 11, 2005; Golden was released on May 25, 2007.

Overview

On the night of March 23, 1998, 11-year-old Andrew Douglas Golden and his friend Mitchell Johnson, age 13, loaded Johnson's mother's van with weapons, snack foods, and camping supplies. The next day, Golden stole his mother's car keys and drove with Johnson to Westside Middle School, where they were students. Johnson parked the van in some woods behind the school. Johnson sat on a hill in the back yard of the school. Golden went inside and pulled the fire alarm, then ran to rejoin Johnson. As students and teachers responded to what they thought was a routine fire alarm and evacuated the building, Johnson and Golden opened fire on them.[156]

The boys fired for four minutes, killing four students and a teacher, and wounding 10 more students. As police arrived on scene, Johnson and Golden ran into the woods to the van. They were caught by pursuing officers and arrested.[157]

EXIT

Panicked students ran screaming back inside the school as classmates were hit by the shooters. "We thought it was just firecrackers," said one student. "I started running towards the gym."[158]

OTHER

Protected/helped

Teachers stood in front of students so that they would feel safe.[159] One teacher stepped back inside and pulled several students with her.[160]

English teacher Shannon Wright threw herself in front of sixth-grader Emma Pittman and was shot twice. Wright died in surgery, but Emma was unharmed.[161]

Case #26 – Thurston High School

Synopsis	Thurston High School student Kipland P. Kinkel, 15, went on a shooting spree, killing his parents at home and two students at school. He was later arrested.
Type of Establishment	School
Environment	Indoors
Motive	Unknown
Number killed	4
Number killed and injured	23
Date of murders	May 21, 1998
Weapons	.22 caliber Ruger semi-automatic rifle; 9mm Glock 19 semi-automatic pistol
Location	Springfield, Oregon
Shooter status	Sentenced on November 10, 1999 to 111 years in prison without the possibility of parole.

Overview

On May 20, 1998, freshman Kip Kinkel was facing expulsion from Thurston High School for being in possession of a handgun. At about 4:00 p.m. he got his father's semi-automatic pistol, loaded it, and went to the kitchen where he shot his father in the back of the head as his father was drinking coffee. His father died instantly.[162] He then waited for his mother to get home from work. When she arrived, Kinkel told her that he loved her, and then shot her repeatedly through the head and heart.[163]

On the following day, May 21, shortly before 8:00 a.m., Kinkel drove to the school, parked a few blocks away, and walked inside carrying a .22 caliber Ruger pistol, and a Glock handgun. Dressed in a trench coat, he ran through the cafeteria, firing his rifle from the hip.[164] By the time the shooting ended, there were two dead and 19 wounded by gunfire. Kinkel had expended 51 rounds.[165]

EXIT/CONCEALMENT

As bullets shattered the cafeteria's plate-glass windows, terrified students ran for cover and dived under tables. Student Stacy Compton said she ducked under a table; her best friend was hit in the forehead.[166]

ENGAGE

Worked together to subdue gunman

Jake Ryker, 17-year-old student wrestler, was bleeding from wounds to his hand and chest. As Kinkel attempted to reload his empty weapon, Ryker tackled him. Several others quickly piled on and helped to hold the gunman until police arrived.[167]

CASE #27 – COLUMBINE HIGH SCHOOL	
Synopsis	Eric Harris, 18, and Dylan Klebold, 17, opened fire throughout Columbine High School before committing suicide.
Historical Note	The Columbine attack was the 5th deadliest school shooting in U.S. history.
Type of Establishment	School
Environment	Outdoors to indoors
Motive	Unknown
Number killed	13
Number killed and injured	37
Date of murders	April 20, 1999
Weapons	***Harris***: 12-gauge Savage Springfield 67H pump-action shotgun; 9mm carbine. ***Klebold***: 9mm TEC-9 semi-automatic handgun; 12-gauge Stevens 311D double-barreled sawed-off shotgun; primarily used the Tec-9 handgun.[168] In addition, they had two 20-lb. propane bombs and a pipe bomb.
Location	Littleton, Colorado
Shooter status	Both committed suicide the same day by shooting themselves.

Overview

On the morning of April 29, 1999, Columbine High School seniors Eric Harris, 18, and Dylan Klebold, 17, arrived at the school separately and met near Harris' car. They armed two 20-pound propane bombs, setting them to explode at 11:17 a.m., and entered the cafeteria just before the A lunch shift began. They then returned to their vehicles to wait for the bombs to explode. When that did not happen, Harris and Klebold armed themselves with their weapons and walked together toward the school. At the top of the west entrance steps they threw a pipe bomb, which exploded.[169]

The two then pulled out their guns from beneath their trench coats and Harris immediately began shooting at two students who were next to the west entrance of the school. He removed his trench coat and shot down the west staircase towards three youths. Harris and Klebold then turned and began shooting south in the direction of five students. Klebold walked down the steps towards the cafeteria, and Harris began to shoot down the steps at several students sitting near the cafeteria's entrance. They shot in the direction of students standing close to a soccer field but did not hit anyone. They then made their way towards the west entrance, throwing pipe bombs as they did so, but none of them detonated.[170]

A Jefferson County Deputy Sheriff arrived on scene within a few minutes and began shooting at Harris and Klebold. The shooters ran inside the school and down the main north hallway, throwing pipe bombs and shooting at any individual they encountered. They proceeded to the library hallway.[171]

At 11:29 a.m., Harris and Klebold entered the library, where a total of 52 students, two teachers and two librarians had concealed themselves. As the shooters approached the library, Harris yelled for everyone to "Get up!" When no one stood up in response, they started moving around and shooting many of those inside. While in the library, Harris and Klebold noticed police evacuating students outside the school, and then they shot out the windows of the library and in the direction of the police, who returned fire.[172]

At approximately 12:08 p.m., Harris and Klebold shouted in unison: "One! Two! Three!" These words were immediately followed by the sound of gunfire. Both had committed suicide: Harris by firing his shotgun through the roof of his mouth; Klebold by shooting himself in the left temple with his TEC-9 semi-automatic handgun.[173]

In the end, 12 students and one teacher were killed; 24 other students were injured as a direct result of the massacre. Three more were injured indirectly as they attempted to escape the school.[174]

EXIT

Student Michael Johnson was hit in the face, leg and arm, yet managed to run from the scene and escaped.[175]

As Coach William David Sanders and a student walked down the Library hallway, they were confronted by both Harris and Klebold. Sanders and the student turned around and ran in the opposite direction; Harris and Klebold shot at both Sanders and the student, hitting Sanders twice in the chest as he reached the south hallway, but missing the student.

Patrick Ireland had lost and regained consciousness several times after being shot by Klebold. He managed to crawl to the library windows, where he reached out and fell into the arms of two SWAT team members standing on the roof of an emergency vehicle.[176]

Before Klebold exited the cafeteria and ascended the staircase to meet Harris, Harris severely wounded and partially paralyzed 17-year-old Anne-Marie Hochhalter as she attempted to flee.[177]

CONCEALMENT

The student who fled with Coach Sanders ran into a classroom where he alerted the others present there to conceal themselves.[178]

Teacher Patti Nielson called emergency services as she also urged students to take cover beneath desks and remain silent. She joined Brian Anderson and three library staff in the exterior break room, into which Klebold had earlier fired shots. They locked themselves in and stayed there until they were freed, at approximately 3:30 p.m.[179]

16-year-old Kyle Velasquez had curled up underneath the computer table. Klebold shot Velasquez, hitting him in the head and back, killing him.[180]

CONCEALMENT/OTHER

Gunman's decision

Harris approached a table where two girls were hiding. He bent down to look at them and dismissed them as "pathetic."[181]

In the center of the library, the killers reloaded their weapons at a table located midway across the room. Harris noticed student John Savage hiding nearby and asked him to identify himself. Savage stated his name and asked Klebold what they were doing, to which Klebold replied: "Oh, just killing people." Savage then asked if they were going to kill him. Klebold hesitated, and then told Savage to leave the library. He fled immediately and escaped through the library's main entrance.[182]

Evan Todd, who had been injured in the outer room of the library, hid behind the administrative counter. When Harris and Klebold headed toward the counter, they discovered Todd. They taunted him and debated killing him, but eventually walked away. Almost immediately, 34 uninjured and 10 injured students evacuated the room through the north door, which led out to the sidewalk adjacent to the west entrance.[183]

On several occasions, the killers looked through the windows of classroom doors and made eye contact with students hiding inside, but neither shooter attempted to enter those rooms. After leaving the main office, Harris and Klebold walked towards a bathroom entrance, where they taunted students hiding inside, saying, "We know you're in there" and "Let's kill anyone we find in here." However, neither one attempted to enter the bathroom.[184]

OTHER

Played dead

Inside the library, 16-year-old Craig Scott hid underneath one table next to Isaiah Shoels and Matthew Kechter. Harris knelt and shot Shoels once in the chest at close range, killing him. Klebold also knelt and opened fire, hitting and killing Kechter. Craig Scott lay next to his friends and played dead and was uninjured.[185]

Student Mark Taylor was shot in the chest, arms and leg and fell to the ground, where he played dead and survived.[186]

OTHER
Pleaded for life

Student Bree Pasquale had sat next to the table rather than trying to hide underneath it since there was not enough room to hide. Harris asked Pasquale if she wanted to die, and the girl responded with a plea for her life.[187]

OTHER
Gunman's decision

When the two shooters approached an empty table where they again reloaded their weapons, student Valeen Schnurr, who had been badly wounded by both gunshot wounds and shrapnel, began to cry out, "Oh, God help me!" In response, Klebold approached her and asked her if she believed in God. Schnurr first replied "no" and then "yes" in an attempt to appease Klebold. Klebold then asked her why; whereupon Schnurr replied that it was because it was what her family believed. He taunted her, reloaded his shotgun, and then walked away.[188]

CONCEALMENT/OTHER
Wounded while helping others

Wounded student Patrick Ireland attempted to provide first aid to another student who had been wounded in the knee. As Ireland attempted help, his head rose above the table and into Klebold's view. Klebold shot Ireland a second time, hitting him twice in the head and once in the foot. Ireland was knocked unconscious but survived.[189]

Case #28 – Day Trading Firms	
Synopsis	Day trader Mark O. Barton, 44, bludgeoned his wife and children to death, then a day later went on a shooting spree through the two day- trading firms where he had made internet investments. After being cornered by police outside a gas station, he committed suicide.
Type of Establishment	Business
Environment	Indoors
Motive	Revenge
Number killed	12
Number killed and injured	25
Date of murders	July 29, 1999
Weapons	9mm Glock handgun; .45 caliber Colt handgun
Location	Atlanta, Georgia
Shooter status	Committed suicide later that day by shooting himself.

Overview

Mark O. Barton was a day trader who had lost at least $100,000 in internet stocks and had been denied trading privileges at one-day trade firm. On July 27 and 28, 1999, he bludgeoned to death his estranged wife and their two young children to "save them from a lifetime of pain."[190] On July 29, he headed to the Momentum Securities brokerage office in Atlanta, where his account had been closed after he was unable to cover his losses.[191] He exchanged pleasantries with employees and told them he wanted to make a few transactions, and said, "It's a bad trading day, and it's about to get worse." He pulled out 9mm and .45 caliber handguns, and then opened fire, killing four people.[192]

Barton then walked across Piedmont Road and began shooting in the All-Tech Investment Group, a day-trading firm in the Piedmont Center building, where he killed five others.[193]

Barton escaped and shot himself to death after a five-hour manhunt when police stopped his van at a gas station.

CONCEALMENT

As arriving police officers searched the Momentum offices, they found several people hiding huddled in a small room near where the victims lay. One of them had thrown a computer out the window to attract the attention of someone on the street.[194]

OTHER

Gunman's decision

Four hours passed before authorities heard from someone who had seen Barton. About the same time, a woman who had been shopping approached her parked car. Barton walked toward her. "Don't scream or I'll shoot you," he said, according to a police report. The woman backed away. Barton told her, “Don’t run or I’ll shoot you.” She ran, and he did not shoot.[195]

Case #29 – Wedgwood Baptist Church

Synopsis	Larry Gene Ashbrook, 47, opened fire inside a church building during a teen church service before committing suicide.
Type of Establishment	Church
Environment	Indoors
Motive	Unknown (mental illness)
Number killed	7
Number killed and injured	14
Date of murders	September 15, 1999
Weapons	9mm semi-automatic handgun; .380 caliber handgun
Location	Fort Worth, Texas
Shooter status	Committed suicide the same day by shooting himself.

Overview

Larry Gene Ashbrook was a loner who had difficulty in keeping a job. His neighbors reported that he exposed himself, screamed obscenities, and kicked doors during fits of rage.[196] In September of 1999 he wrote two letters to the editor of the Fort Worth Star-Telegram complaining about the CIA, psychological warfare, assaults by co-workers, being drugged by police and being suspected of being a serial killer, and repeated the concerns in a phone call to a local alternative newspaper. "No one will listen to me," he said. "No one will believe me."[197]

On September 15, Ashbrook entered the Wedgwood Baptist Church in Fort Worth during a service for teens and young adults. He asked one person "What's the program? Then he shot a janitor who approached him and killed two other people before walking into the sanctuary.[198]

Cursing and shouting anti-Baptist rhetoric, Ashbrook opened fire with a 9mm semi-automatic handgun and a .380 caliber handgun. He reloaded several times during the shooting; three empty magazines were found at the scene. He then sat down on a back pew and shot and killed himself.[199]

Three adults and four teens were killed, and seven were wounded.

EXIT/CONCEALMENT

The teens present in the sanctuary thought at first that Ashbrook's entrance and shouting was part of a skit. When he opened fire, they scrambled for cover.[200]

"We were singing a song and then in the middle of the song this guy opened the door and fired one shot," Chris Applegate said. "He just kept telling us to stay still." "We all just jumped under the benches and he fired about 10 more shots. ... Somebody said, 'Run, run,' and we all started running."[201]

Case #30 – Xerox Corp.

Synopsis	Byran Koji Uyesugi, 40, a Xerox service technician, opened fire inside his office building. He fled and was apprehended after a five-hour standoff with police.
Type of Establishment	Workplace
Environment	Indoors
Motive	Revenge
Number killed	7
Number killed and injured	7
Date of murders	November 2, 1999
Weapons	9mm Glock handgun
Location	Honolulu, Hawaii
Shooter status	Sentenced to life in prison without parole on August 8, 2000.

Overview

Byran Koji Uyesugi began working for Xerox as a service technician in 1984. After years on the job, he was transferred to another work group. He began making accusations of harassment and product tampering about fellow repairmen. He was hostile to co-workers and alienated customers, and his work performance was below par. He began leaving threatening notes to his coworkers.[202]

Xerox management had decided to phase out the copier that Uyesugi serviced and replace it with a new machine, which Uyesugi did not want to learn. On November 1, 1999, his manager notified him that he would begin training on it the next day.

On the morning of November 2, Uyesugi reported to work and went to the second floor. He opened fire with a 9mm Glock, killing his supervisor and six co-workers and firing in the direction of another co-worker who fled the building. He killed seven male employees. After the shooting, Uyesugi fled in a company van.[203]

Police closed down several streets in downtown Honolulu as they investigated the crime scene. By mid-morning, the police had Uyesugi cornered in the mountains above downtown Honolulu. After a nearly five-hour standoff, Uyesugi surrendered to police.[204]

ENGAGE

Jason Balatico charged toward Uyesugi to wrestle the gun away, but Uyesugi fired a "hail of shots" at him, downing him with five shots.[205]

OTHER

Passed over by gunman

Lance Hamura spoke briefly to Uyesugi on the first floor before the Uyesugi embarked on his rampage on the floor above. Uyesugi walked past Ronald Yamanaka, who was having coffee in a second-floor break room, and went to a computer room at the end of the hall where two other co-workers were. He aimed the gun directly at Ron Kawamae's head and pulled the trigger.[206]

Case #31 – Radisson Bay Harbor Hotel	
Synopsis	Hotel employee Silvio Izquierdo-Leyva, 36, gunned down four co-workers at the Radisson Bay Harbor Hotel before killing a woman outside in an attempted carjacking.
Type of Establishment	Hotel
Environment	Indoors/outdoors
Motive	Revenge
Number killed	5
Number killed and injured	8
Date of murders	December 30, 1999
Weapons	Two handguns
Location	Tampa, Florida
Shooter status	Sentenced to life in prison without parole April 15, 2002.

Overview

Cuban immigrant Silvio Izquierdo-Leyva, 36, had worked as a house-keeper at the Radisson Bay Harbor Hotel for only a few months. His sister-in-law Angela Vazquez was employed there as housekeeping supervisor.[207]

On December 30, 1999, Izquierdo-Leyva entered the hotel lobby and opened fire at Vazquez and her daughter standing next to her, but missed. He chased Vazquez through the halls, and went outside. He pointed his gun at Rafael Barrios, a bellman, who had just pulled up in his car. The gun was empty, and as Izquierdo-Leyva stopped to reload, Barrios jumped from his car and ran.

Izquierdo-Leyva went back into the hotel and started shooting again. Then he fled in Barrios' car which was outside the hotel entrance. He abandoned that vehicle and pointed a handgun at a woman driving a sedan. When the woman didn't comply with his demand for the car, he shot her. She began to back up the car, and the gunman moved on to another car. He shot at a Jeep on the street and hit the vehicle, but the driver was able to speed away. The gunman tried for another vehicle and rejected it, then spotted a station wagon heading toward him. As the driver came to a stop, the gunman stepped up to the car, pointing his gun, and the driver surrendered it without incident.

As he drove, Izquierdo was later surrounded by police cars a few blocks away and arrested.

Four of the five people that police said Izquierdo killed were employees of the hotel.[208] The fifth victim, 56-year-old Dolores Perdomo, was the woman shot as Izquierdo attempted to steal her car.[209]

EXIT

"I heard two pops and saw people running out of the hotel," said Carson Woods. "I knew I had to get out of there."[210]

Kenny Sobaski said, "Employees from the hotel came in and said 'Get out! Get out!" [211]

COVER

"I was in the lobby getting my paycheck when I heard shots," Diana Izquierdo said. "My mother and I hid in an office, and I saw Silvio walk by the office door." [212]

OTHER

Refused to comply

The assailant tried to carjack the vehicle driven by 56-year-old Dolores Perdomo. He aimed his handgun at her, and said, "Lady, give me the car." When she didn't comply, he shot her through the driver's side window.[213]

OTHER

Complied

Angel Marteliz was heading home, listening to an afternoon radio talk show. The gunman stepped from the curb as Marteliz came to a stop. He pointed his gun at Marteliz. "Take the car," Marteliz said as he stepped out. "Thank you," the gunman replied. "I knew to give him the car," Marteliz said later. "I didn't argue."[214]

OTHER

Gunman's choice

Guest Robyn Gerber, a basketball team member in town for a bowl game, came face to face with the gunman as she tried to flee. "He told Robyn he wasn't interested in (shooting) anyone else, the team was OK," reported a teammate's father.[215]

CASE STUDIES – 2000s

CASE #32 – EDGEWATER TECHNOLOGY OFFICE

Synopsis	Michael McDermott, 42, opened fire on co-workers and was later arrested.
Type of Establishment	Workplace
Environment	Indoors
Motive	Revenge
Number killed	7
Number killed and injured	7
Date of murders	December 26, 2000
Weapons	AK-47-type semi-automatic rifle; 12-gauge shotgun; .32 caliber semi-automatic pistol
Location	Wakefield, Massachusetts
Shooter status	In 2002, sentenced to seven consecutive life sentences without possibility of parole.

Overview

Michael McDermott was an application support employee for Edgewater Technology in Wakefield, Massachusetts. He had been levied by the IRS for back taxes, and his employer had been asked to garnish his wages for the tax levy.[216]

On December 26, 2000, carrying a semi-automatic rifle, a shotgun, and a pistol, McDermott entered the Edgewater office. A coworker asked, "Where are you going with that?" and he responded, "Human Resources." McDermott shot to death two employees in the reception area, and then headed to the hallway, where he killed three people. When he got to the accounting office he found the door locked. After shooting out the lock with a shotgun blast, he killed two people inside the room.

McDermott then returned to the lobby, sat in a chair within reach of a black tote bag packed with ammunition, and waited for the police. When police found him, he was sitting calmly and stated that he didn't speak German.[217]

CONCEALMENT

Another employee in the accounting office survived by concealing herself underneath a desk. [218]

OTHER

Specific targets

The Middlesex County District Attorney noted that the shootings appeared to have been "targeted at the individuals, rather than indiscriminate spraying of gunfire." The victims were at their work stations... The whole thing took between five and 10 minutes." [219]

Case #33 – Navistar International Engine Plant

Synopsis	Fired employee William D. Baker, 66, opened fire at his former workplace before committing suicide.
Type of Establishment	Workplace
Environment	Indoors
Motive	Revenge
Number killed	4
Number killed and injured	8
Date of murders	February 5, 2001
Weapons	AK-47 assault rifle
Location	DuPage County, Illinois
Shooter status	Committed suicide the same day by shooting himself.

Overview

William D. Baker had been employed by Navistar as a forklift operator for nearly 40 years before being fired in 1995 for stealing engine parts. In January 2001, he was convicted in federal court of conspiracy to commit interstate theft, and was scheduled to begin a five-month prison sentence on February 6 and to pay a $195,000 fine.[220]

On the morning of February 5, Baker showed up at the Navistar plant carrying weapons in a golf bag. He approached a security guard and said that he had some "personal belongings" to give to a coworker. When the guard refused him entry and said she would have the friend come to meet him outside the building, Baker pointed a revolver at her and forced her to let him in the building.

Baker walked through the plant's diesel-engine testing room and fired at workers in his way. His actions appeared to be random, not targeting any specific individuals. He shot seven people in the engineering area, three of them fatally. After firing 25 to 30 rounds, he walked into a corner office, shot and killed his last victim, and then shot himself in the head with a handgun.[221] The rampage lasted no more than 15 minutes.

EXIT

24-year-old engineer Martin Reutimann was sitting at his desk when he heard gunfire about 10:00 a.m. "I heard somebody yell, 'There's a guy in the center aisle with a gun!'" Reutimann said. Seeing people running past him, Reutimann grabbed his coat and cell phone, and dialed 911.[222]

Case #34 – Lockheed Martin Plant	
Synopsis	Assembly line worker Douglas Williams, 48, opened fire at his workplace before committing suicide.
Type of Establishment	Workplace
Environment	Indoors
Motive	Rage
Number killed	6
Number killed and injured	14
Date of murders	July 3, 2003
Weapons	12-gauge shotgun; mini 14 .223 semi-automatic rifle
Location	Meridian, Mississippi
Shooter status	Committed suicide the same day by shooting himself.

Overview

Douglas Williams, a factory worker known as a "hothead" who was "mad at the world"[223] and talked about "murdering others,"[224]opened fire with a shotgun at the Lockheed Martin plant where he worked. Wearing a black tee shirt and camouflage pants and carrying a bandolier of ammunition, Williams entered the building with what is believed to have been two weapons, a .12-gauge shotgun and a mini 14 .223 caliber semi-automatic weapon. There were additional weapons found later in his truck. After killing six fellow employees, Williams committed suicide.

EXIT

Dozens of employees ran for cover, screaming "Get out! Get out!" after Williams started firing.[225]

Assembly worker Booker Stevenson said, "...I walked to the aisle and saw him aiming his gun. I took off. Everybody took off."[226]

Case #35 – Damageplan Concert	
Synopsis	Nathan Gale, 25, gunned down musician Darrell "Dimebag" Abbott and three others at a *Damageplan* show before a police officer fatally shot Gale.
Type of Establishment	Concert
Environment	Indoors
Motive	Undetermined
Number killed	4
Number killed and injured	7
Date of murders	December 8, 2004
Weapons	9mm Beretta handgun
Location	Columbus, Ohio
Shooter status	Killed by police

Overview

Nathan Gale was a 6'5", 268-pound former Marine who had been discharged in October 2003. His mother and former employer later said that Gale told them he was discharged due to a diagnosis of paranoid schizophrenia, but he had no previous history of violence.[227]

Gale was a huge fan of the heavy metal band Damageplan, which was scheduled to perform a concert in the Alrosa Villa Club in Columbus, Ohio. By the time the band came onstage to perform shortly after 10:00 p.m., there were at least 400 people in the club.

The band was playing its opening song when Gale suddenly emerged from behind a bank of amplifiers and headed across the stage toward Dimebag. He pulled a handgun and fired three shots at close range into the back of the guitarist's head, and another that struck his hand.[228]

Fans and club employees began rushing the stage in an attempt to stop the attack; Gale turned his gun on them.

Columbus police officer James Niggemeyer had just started his shift at the precinct two miles away when the first report came of shots fired at the club. He grabbed his shotgun and entered the club through the stage door. Coming face to face with Gale, he fired and killed him.[229]

EXIT

After the first shots, at 10:18 p.m., an Alrosa Villa employee fled from the club to call the police.[230]

Band vocalist Patrick Lachman shouted, "Call 911!" into his microphone, and then jumped offstage.[231]

ENGAGE

Before Gale could fire again, security guard Jeff Thompson rushed at him. Thompson died after being shot twice in the body and once in the leg.[232]

Erin Halk was a member of the band's security staff. He attempted to engage the killer, and charged when Gale was reloading. He was shot and died at the scene.[233]

Other people rushed from the wings and over the barricades onto the stage, either to help Dimebag or to try to subdue the shooter. Gale then took drum tech John Brooks hostage, holding him in a headlock position after Brooks tried to wrestle the gunman to the ground.[234]

OTHER

Drew attention of shooter

Fan Nathan Bray was attempting to administer CPR to Abbott and band security chief Jeffery Thompson when he stopped, turned around and looked at Gale, with both arms out, palms up. Gale shot and killed him.[235]

Case #36 – Living Church of God	
Synopsis	Church member Terry Michael Ratzmann, 44, opened fire at a church meeting at a hotel before committing suicide.
Type of Establishment	Church
Environment	Undetermined
Motive	Indoors
Number killed	7
Number killed and injured	11
Date of murders	March 12, 2005
Weapons	9mm handgun
Location	Brookfield, Wisconsin
Shooter status	Committed suicide the same day by shooting himself.

Overview

Terry Michael Ratzmann was on the verge of losing his job as a computer technician, reportedly suffered from bouts of depression, and had a drinking problem. A member of the Living Church of God in Brookfield, Wisconsin, Ratzmann was reportedly angered by a sermon which the minister had given two weeks earlier.[236]

On March 12, 2005 Ratzmann left the room in the Sheraton Hotel where the congregation held its services. He returned 20 minutes later, carrying his 9mm handgun, and walked up and down the rows of chairs, firing 22 rounds, killing the minister, the minister's son, and five others.[237]

During the shooting he reportedly spoke aloud to the congregation, telling them that he had brought three magazines of ammunition and intended to kill the entire congregation. Midway through the second magazine, Ratzmann shot and killed himself.[238]

CONCEALMENT

Chandra Frazier dove under a chair. "I just remember crawling on the carpet and just praying, screaming out and praying," Frazier. The man sitting in the chair was killed.[239]

OTHER

Questioned gunman

One of Ratzmann's friends begged him to stop, calling him by name and saying, "Stop, stop, why?" Ratzmann did not reply but fired a few more rounds before fatally shooting himself.[240]

Case #37 – Red Lake High School

Synopsis	Jeffrey Weise, 16, murdered his police officer grandfather and his grandfather's girlfriend, then drove to Red Lake Senior High School on the Red Lake Indian reservation and opened fire, killing another seven people before committing suicide.
Historical Note	The Red Lake massacre was the deadliest tribal school shooting in U.S. history.
Type of Establishment	School
Environment	Indoors
Motive	Unknown
Number killed	9
Number killed and injured	16
Date of murders	March 21, 2005
Weapons	9mm Glock; pump-action shotgun
Location	Red Lake, Minnesota
Shooter status	Committed suicide the same day by shooting himself.

Overview

Red Lake High School student Jeffrey Weise was a loner who often wore black, and was teased by other students. His father had committed suicide, and his mother was a resident of a nursing home due to brain injuries suffered in a car accident.[241] Weise had been receiving mental health counseling and medication for depression.[242]

On the afternoon of March 21, 2005, Jeffrey shot his grandfather, Daryl Lussier, with a .22 pistol while Lussier was sleeping. He is believed to have stolen Lussier's two police-issue weapons, a 9mm Glock and a pump-action shotgun. Weise shot Michele Sigana, Lussier's girlfriend and police partner, when she returned home.[243]

Weise then drove a patrol vehicle (believed to be his grandfather's) to the high school building. Passing through the building's main entrance, he encountered unarmed security guard Derrick Brun who was manning the school's metal detector. Weise fatally shot Brun, and then proceeded down a hallway while firing, killing five students and a teacher and injuring seven others.[244]

When police officers arrived, they exchanged gunfire with Weise, who then apparently retreated to a classroom and killed himself. The entire episode lasted about 10 minutes.[245] All of the dead students, including the killer, were found in one room.[246]

COVER

During the shootings, teachers led students from one room to another in an effort to move away from the sound of the shooting.[247]

One quick-thinking teacher locked the classroom door and thwarted Weise's attempt to enter.[248]

OTHER

Played dead

15-year-old Lance Crowe survived by playing dead, lying among those killed. From the floor, Crowe watched as the shooter came back into the classroom and killed himself just a few feet away as the police closed in.[249]

Case #38 – Mail Processing Center

Synopsis	Former postal worker Jennifer San Marco, 44, shot dead a former neighbor and then drove to the mail processing plant where she had worked and opened fire, killing six employees before committing suicide.
Type of Establishment	Post Office
Environment	Indoors
Motive	Revenge
Number killed	7
Number killed and injured	7
Date of murders	January 30, 2006
Weapons	15-round 9mm pistol
Location	Goleta, California
Shooter status	Committed suicide the same day by shooting herself.

Overview

Jennifer San Marco had a history of bizarre behavior, according to those who knew her. She carried on conversations with herself and rummaged through dumpsters. She had made racist comments to coworkers, and in 2004 expressed the intent to start a publication called "The Racist Press." She was a loner with no known family or friends.[250] San Marco's mental problems were the apparent reason for her retirement on medical leave after six years of employment at the mail processing center in Goleta, California.[251]

On January 30, 2006, San Marco shot and killed her former neighbor, Beverly Graham, and then drove to her former place of employment, the mail processing plant, about 9:00 p.m. She drove through a gate behind another car and then took an employee's identification badge at gunpoint. She shot two people in the parking lot before entering the building and shooting four more. She then took her own life.[252]

Authorities said it was unclear whether San Marco targeted specific employees at the postal center, but a postal inspector said "chances are" she knew the people she was shooting at.[253]

EXIT

About 80 of the approximately 300 people who work at the mail-sorting center were on hand when San Marco arrived. Authorities said that many of them fled to a fire station across the street when the shooting began.[254]

OTHER

Complied

San Marco gained entry to the building by taking an employee's identification badge at gunpoint. That worker was not hurt.[255]

Case #39 – Rave After-party	
Synopsis	Kyle Aaron Huff, 28, opened fire at a rave after-party in the Capitol Hill neighborhood of Seattle before committing suicide.
Type of Establishment	Residence
Environment	Outdoors to indoors
Motive	Unknown
Number killed	6
Number killed and injured	8
Date of murders	March 25, 2006
Weapons	12-gauge Winchester shotgun; 40-caliber semi-automatic Ruger handgun
Location	Seattle, Washington
Shooter status	Committed suicide the same day by shooting himself.

Overview

Kyle Aaron Huff was a former pizza delivery man and an art student who was one of the first to arrive at an early morning “after party” following a rave in Seattle, Washington. The party was held in a house in a quiet residential area called Capitol Hill. Huff kept to himself, was quiet and polite, and made friendly small talk with others present.[256]

Close to 7:00 a.m., Huff left the house and went to his truck parked nearby. He retrieved a 12-gauge pistol-grip Winchester Defender shotgun and a .40 caliber semi-automatic Ruger handgun, more than 300 rounds worth of ammunition, and a can of spray paint.[257]

Huff spray-painted the word "NOW" on the sidewalk and on the steps of a neighboring home, and then pulled out the handgun. He walked up to a landing near the front porch of the party house and opened fire.[258] Huff fired repeatedly as he proceeded through the house, killing four men and two women.

Officer Steve Leonard, patrolling in the neighborhood, heard shots fired and went to the scene. When Huff emerged carrying a shotgun, Leonard ordered him to put down the weapon. Huff turned the gun on himself and fired a fatal shot.[259] The shooting inside the house had lasted only minutes.

EXIT

People fled the house, some through the back door and others out the windows. A neighbor living across the street heard six shots, looked out his window, and saw people scattering from the home.[260]

COVER

Alissa Dunn and Gary Will were in an upstairs bathroom. When they heard the shots, they locked the door and hid in the bathtub. Huff fired a round through the door, missing the couple crouching in the tub.[261]

CONCEALMENT

"He randomly came up, fired, and people scrambled to find a hiding place, said one of those inside the house.[262]

One person hid under a bed and saw the shooter's feet as he walked into the room. He heard Huff say, "I've got enough ammunition to shoot everybody."[263]

A 911 dispatcher asked a female caller if the shooter was still there. "I don't know," a hushed, frightened voice says. "We're hiding."[264]

Huff also went down into the basement, where three men were hiding.[265]

OTHER

Bystander Responses

At least one of the 911 calls came from inside the house. Other calls were made by neighbors. Neighbor Albert Sbragia heard the shots and looked out his bedroom window. He saw Huff firing at the front of the house. His wife Dawn called 911 and told her children to lie down on the floor. Across the street, William Lowe heard shots and called 911.

Cesar Clemente woke up to the sound of gunshots. After calling 911, he went to his door and saw two injured people fleeing into bushes. "You guys come over here," he said. One man, shot in the arm and side, made it across the street and into Clemente's home. The other person collapsed in the bushes.[266]

CASE #40 – NICKEL MINES AMISH SCHOOL	
Synopsis	Charles Carl Roberts, 32, shot 10 young girls in a one-room Amish schoolhouse, killing five, before taking his own life.
Type of Establishment	School
Environment	Indoors
Motive	Unknown
Number killed	5
Number killed and injured	10
Date of murders	October 2, 2006
Weapons	9mm semi-automatic pistol; 12-gauge shotgun; rifle
Location	Bart Township, Pennsylvania
Shooter status	Committed suicide the same day by shooting himself.

Overview

Charles Carl Roberts was a milk tank truck driver who lived in the town of Bart in Lancaster County, Pennsylvania. On October 2, 2006, he armed himself with a 9mm semi-automatic pistol, a 12-gauge shotgun and a rifle, along with a bag of some 600 rounds of ammunition, two cans of smokeless powder, two knives, and a stun gun, along with rolls of tape, some tools, and a change of clothes.[267]

Roberts drove to the West Nickel Mines School, a one-room Amish schoolhouse, and entered at just before 10:00 a.m. He sent the boys and adults outside, and then barricaded the doors with lumber nailed into place. He bound the girls' feet with wire and plastic ties and lined them up along the chalkboard, then opened fire.[268]

Roberts had called his wife from a cell phone shortly before the shooting began, saying he was acting out in revenge for something that happened 20 years ago. Once police were able to enter the school, they found Roberts dead of a self-inflicted gunshot wound.[269]

Roberts appeared to have no grudge against the Amish community and may have picked the school because it was nearby and had little or no security.[270]

EXIT

Nine-year-old Emma Fisher escaped in the beginning; her two older sisters stayed inside.[271]

OTHER

Gunman's decision

Initially the gunman released all 15 male students present, along with a pregnant woman and three parents with infants.[272]

OTHER

Pleaded for life

The oldest girl, 13-year-old Marian Fisher, appealed to Roberts to shoot her first, apparently in an effort to spare the younger girls. Her younger sister Barbie appealed to Roberts to shoot her next. She received bullet wounds in the hand, leg, and shoulder but survived.[273]

Case #41 – Trolley Square Mall	
Synopsis	Sulejman Talović, 18, rampaged through a shopping center until he was shot dead by police.
Type of Establishment	Shopping mall
Environment	Indoors
Motive	Unknown
Number killed	5
Number killed and injured	9
Date of murders	February 12, 2007
Weapon	Shotgun; .38 caliber pistol
Location	Salt Lake City, Utah
Shooter status	Shot dead by police the same day.

Overview

Bosnian immigrant Sulejman Talović, 18, lived in Salt Lake City with his mother. Neighbors seldom saw him, and he was considered a loner. He was enrolled in several city schools before withdrawing in 2004.[274]

On February 12, 2007, Talović took a backpack full of ammunition, a shotgun, and a .38 caliber pistol, and went to the Trolley Square shopping mall in Salt Lake City. Stepping out of his car, he immediately began shooting, firing at anyone in his line of sight.[275] He killed two people, then a third as he came through a door. Five others were shot inside a gift shop.[276]

Kenneth Hammond, an off-duty police officer, was at the mall for dinner with his wife. When he realized what was happening, he drew his gun and told his wife to call the police. He fired on Talović, drawing the gunman's attention until other officers could arrive. "I've been in situations before where I've had to chase a guy who was pointing a gun at me," Hammond said, "I feel like I was there and did what I had to do."[277]

After Talović was cornered and shooting at officers, an active shooter contact team comprised of Salt Lake City Police Department SWAT team members arrived and shot him.[278]

CONCEALMENT

Marie Smith, a store manager, said she had seen the gunman through the store window. “He didn’t seem upset, or like he was on a rampage,” she said. She crawled to an employee restroom to hide with others.[279]

Matt Lund was visiting his wife who was manager of the Secret Garden children's clothing store, when he heard the first shots. The couple and three others hid in a storage room for about 40 minutes, still able to hear the violence.[280]

Barb McKeown, 60, was in an antiques shop when two frantic women ran in and reported gunshots. "Then we heard shot after shot after shot," said McKeown. She and three others hid under a staircase until it was safe to leave.[281]

For hours after the rampage had ended, police searched stores for frightened shoppers and employees who were still in hiding, waiting for safe escort from the scene.[282]

OTHER

Warned others

One of the wounded shoppers, Shawn Munns, was alone outside the mall after a meal with his wife and two stepchildren when Talović blasted him with a shotgun. With dozens of pellets embedded in his side, Munns staggered into a nearby café and warned diners about the gunman, and told them to lock the doors.[283]

CASE #42 – VIRGINIA TECH UNIVERSITY

Synopsis	Virginia Tech student Seung-Hui Cho, 29, opened fire on his school's campus before committing suicide.
Historical note	The Virginia Tech massacre was the deadliest school shooting in modern U.S. history.
Type of Establishment	University campus
Environment	Indoors
Motive	Unknown (mental illness)
Number killed	32
Number killed and injured	61
Date of murders	April 16, 2007
Weapons	.22 caliber Walther P22 semi-automatic pistol; 9mm Glock 19 semi-automatic pistol
Location	Blacksburg, Virginia
Shooter status	Committed suicide the same day by shooting himself.

Overview

Seung-Hui Cho was a South Korean who had moved to the U.S. at the age of eight. In middle school he was diagnosed with a severe anxiety disorder as well as major depressive disorder. He received therapy and treatment until his junior year of high school. [284] In 2007 he was a senior majoring in English at Virginia Tech. There, he had a history of incidents including allegations of stalking, had referrals to counseling, and several of his writings caused concern among classmates and teachers.[285]

At about 7:15 a.m. in West Ambler Johnston Hall, a dorm, Cho shot and killed two students. He returned to his room and re-armed himself, and mailed a package containing pictures, digital files, and documents, to NBC News.[ii] At close to 10:00 a.m., police responded to a 911 call reporting that shots had been fired at Norris Hall, a building about a half-mile away on the opposite side of the campus. They found that the building's front doors had been chained from the inside, so that no one could exit and police could not enter.[286]

Cho entered classroom after classroom and shot people at random. He killed 25 students and five faculty members, and wounded 29 in Norris Hall, where police reports indicate that Cho fired about 170 rounds. Officers forced their way into the building and followed the sound of gunshots to the second floor. As police began closing in on Cho, he shot and killed himself.[287]

EXIT

As Cho proceeded through Norris Hall shooting, students leapt to safety from the windows of their classrooms.[288]

COVER

Hearing the commotion on the floor below, Kevin Granata and Wally Grant brought 20 students from a nearby classroom into an office where the door could be locked.[289]

ENGAGE

Air Force ROTC student Matthew LaPorte, is reported to have attempted to tackle Cho from behind but was fatally injured in the attempt.[290]

OTHER

Tried to help others

Several people tried to help others during the attack. Around 9:30 am, a student walked into Room 211 at Norris Hall and alerted the occupants that a shooting had occurred at West Ambler Johnston.[291]

[ii] In the media package sent to NBC, Cho discussed "martyrs like Eric and Dylan," apparently referring to the Columbine High School gunmen. The Virginia Tech massacre occurred just four days before the eight-year-anniversary of the Columbine shooting.

OTHER

Barricaded doors

Professor Liviu Librescu held the door of his classroom shut while Cho attempted to enter the room, and was able to keep Cho out until the students had escaped through the windows. The professor was eventually shot five times and killed. Professor Couture-Nowak looked Cho in the eye in the hallway. She ordered her students to the back of the classroom for their safety and made a fatal attempt to barricade the door.[292]

Around 9:40 a.m., students in Norris 205 heard gunshots. The students barricaded the door with a large table, while Cho shot several times through the door. No one in that classroom was killed.[293]

Several students barricaded the door of Room 207 after the first attack and helped the wounded. Cho returned minutes later, but students Derek O'Dell and Katelyn Carney prevented him from re-entering; both were injured.[294]

OTHER

Drew attention of shooter

Waleed Shaalan, a teaching assistant and student from Egypt, although wounded, distracted Cho from a nearby student after the shooter had returned to the room. Shaalan was shot a second time and died.[295]

Partahi Lumbantoruan protected fellow student Guillermo Colman by diving on top of him. Lumbantoruan was killed by gunshots, but Colman was protected by Lumbantoruan's body.[296]

CONCEALMENT/EXIT

Left hiding place

Kevin Granata and Wally Grant left the locked room and went down-stairs to investigate. Both were shot by Cho. Grant was wounded and survived, but Granata died from his injuries. None of the students locked in Granata's office were injured.[297]

Case #43 – Apartment Building	
Synopsis	Off-duty sheriff's deputy Tyler Peterson, 20, opened fire inside an apartment where his ex-girlfriend and friends were gathered for a movie-watching party. He later committed suicide.
Type of Establishment	Residence
Environment	Indoors
Motive	Domestic dispute
Number killed	6
Number killed and injured	7
Date of murders	October 7, 2007
Weapons	AR-15 rifle; pistol
Location	Crandon, Wisconsin
Shooter status	Committed suicide the same day by shooting himself.

Overview

Tyler Peterson had just been hired as a deputy in the Forest County Sheriff's Department and was a part-time officer at the Crandon Police Department in Crandon, Wisconsin.

At about 2:30 a.m. on the morning of October 7, 2007, he entered an apartment complex where a group of friends ages 14 to 20 had been eating pizza and watching movies. One of those present was Peterson's ex-girlfriend, Jordanne Murray, with whom Peterson engaged in a loud argument. She demanded that Peterson leave.[298]

Peterson went to his truck, got his police-issued AR-15 rifle, went back to the party and opened fire. He killed six of those present.[299]

The first officer who responded to the shooting was shot at, but his wounds were superficial from glass fragments. Peterson drove away and went to the house of some friends, where he confessed what he had done. His friends were unable to convince him to turn himself in. He left without harming them.[300]

Authorities were able to establish contact with Peterson and talked with him about surrendering. He went into some nearby woods with his pistol, where he committed suicide by shooting himself in the head.

OTHER

Played dead

One of the partygoers survived because he played dead after being shot three times.[301]

Case #44 – Westroads Mall	
Synopsis	Robert A. Hawkins, 19, opened fire inside a mall before committing suicide.
Type of Establishment	Department store
Environment	Indoors
Motive	Uncertain
Number killed	8
Number killed and injured	13
Date of murders	December 5, 2007
Weapon	AK-47 semi-automatic rifle
Location	Omaha, Nebraska
Shooter status	Committed suicide the same day by shooting himself.

Overview

Robert A. Hawkins had been fired from his job at McDonald's, and had recently broken up with his girlfriend. He had a felony drug conviction and several misdemeanor cases filed against him, including having been arrested in November of 2007 for being a minor in possession of alcohol. He was scheduled to appear in court in December.[302]

On December 5, Hawkins took an AK-47 7.62x39mm semi-automatic rifle, apparently stolen from his stepfather's house, along with two 30-round magazines, concealed in a sweatshirt, into a Nebraska department store, took the elevator up to the third floor, and opened fire on customers and store employees. He killed eight people and wounded five, then turned the gun on himself and killed himself.

Hawkins left a suicide note that said, in part, "sorry for everything," that he did not want to be a burden any longer," that he was worthless, and "Now I'll be famous."[303]

EXIT

Witness Shawn Vidlak said the shots sounded like a nail gun, and thought it was noise from construction work. "People started screaming about gunshots," he said. "I grabbed my wife and kids. We got out of there as fast as we could." [304]

Witnesses described chaos and shoppers frantically running away from the Von Maur store, where the shooting began.[305]

CONCEALMENT

Some shoppers and mall employees ran to hide in clothes racks, dressing rooms, and bathrooms after hearing the shots.[306]

Kristy Wright realized what was happening and yelled "There's a shooter." She tried to turn and run; her friend was frozen in fear. They went to a nearby store, told the employees what had happened and asked if they could hide there. A manager led Wright and others to a room in the back of the store." [307]

"I saw employees taking a bunch of people into the dressing room, but I didn't want to go," shopper Jennifer Kramer said, "I didn't know if this guy was going to come looking for people in dressing rooms, so we hid in a pants rack towards the back of the men's department." [308]

Von Maur employee Keith Fidler said he huddled in the corner of the men's clothing department with about a dozen other employees until police yelled to get out of the store. Another employee who worked in the store's third-floor service department heard shots and went with coworkers and customers into a back closet, emerging about a half-hour later when police shouted to come out with their hands up.[309]

Case #45 – City Council Meeting	
Synopsis	Charles Lee Thornton, 52, went on a rampage at city hall before being shot and killed by police.
Type of Establishment	Government facility
Environment	Outdoors to indoors
Motive	Revenge
Number killed	5
Number killed and injured	7
Date of murders	February 7, 2008
Weapons	.44 magnum revolver; 40 caliber handgun
Location	Kirkwood, Missouri
Shooter status	Killed the same day during a shootout with police.

Overview

Charles Lee Thornton was a lifelong resident of Meacham Park, an unincorporated section of St. Louis County, Missouri. In 1992 commercial development was planned for the community; Thornton received some of the development work for his construction company, but was apparently resentful that he did not receive as much as he wanted. In 1999 he filed a complaint with the Equal Employment Opportunity Commission alleging racial discrimination in the awarding of contracts.[310]

Beginning in 1996 Thornton began receiving citations for various code violations. By May 2002, he had received at least 100 tickets, and had been ordered to pay nearly $20,000 in fines and court costs.[311] He had filed for bankruptcy in December 1999 but failed to comply with his repayment plan; he also never paid any of the code violation fines. He regularly appeared at city council meetings complaining of persecution, fraud and cover-up by city officials.

On May 13, 2002, Thornton was convicted of assault on the city's public works director.[iii] He was also arrested and handcuffed at two city council meetings in 2006, charged with disorderly conduct. There were other instances of misdemeanor charges and public misconduct in subsequent years.

On February 7, 2008, armed with a revolver, Thornton went to city hall where the City Council was meeting. He shot and killed police officer Sgt. William Biggs, who was walking across the street, then took the officer's .40 caliber handgun and entered city hall. Reaching Council chambers, he shot a police officer in the head, then moved on to shoot at close range the public works director, two council members, the mayor, and a reporter. In total, the gunman killed five and wounded two others.[312]

The gunfire was audible to the police department across the street, and two officers rushed to council chambers. Thornton fired on them from behind a desk; they returned fire and Thornton was killed.[313]

ENGAGE/EXIT

In council chambers Thornton chased City Attorney John Hessel, who slowed the gunman by throwing chairs at him until Hessel could escape.[314]

[iii] Yost became one of Thornton's murder victims.

CASE #46 – NORTHERN ILLINOIS UNIVERSITY

Synopsis	Steven Kazmierczak, 28, opened fire in a university lecture hall, then shot and killed himself before police arrived.
Type of Establishment	University
Environment	Indoors
Motive	Unknown
Number killed	5
Number killed and injured	23
Date of murders	February 14, 2008
Weapons	Remington 870 shotgun; 9mm Glock handgun; 9mm Sig Sauer handgun; .380 Hi-Point handgun
Location	DeKalb, Illinois
Shooter status	Committed suicide the same day by shooting himself.

Overview

Steven Kazmierczak was a former student at Northern Illinois University (NIU) who "...had a very good academic record, no record of trouble," according to NIU President John G. Peters.[315] While at NIU, he wrote a paper called "No Crazies With Guns," in which he used the April 2007 Virginia Tech massacre to analyze whether mentally ill people should have access to guns.

Kazmierczak had a history of attempted suicides and was hospitalized nine times for psychiatric issues before 2001.[316] He was discharged from the U.S. Army before completion of basic training for lying about his mental illness. In 2008, according to his girlfriend, he had been taking Xanax (an anti-anxiety medication), Ambien (a sleep aid), and Prozac (an antidepressant), all prescribed by a psychiatrist.[317] In early 2008, Kazmierczak's behavior seemed to be more erratic.

At approximately 3:00 p.m. on February 14, 2008, Kazmierczak, carrying a guitar case, entered a lecture hall in Cole Hall on the NIU campus. The hall contained 150 to 200 students in an oceanography class. The door Kazmierczak used led directly to the stage in front of the room. He removed a Remington 870 shotgun from the guitar case and three handguns from under his coat, and began firing into the crowd of students. Five students were killed and 18 were wounded.[318]

John Giovanni, 20, and others said the gunman aimed at the center of the auditorium. "He just fires right into the audience," Giovanni said. "He didn't say a word. It didn't look like he was aiming directly at someone. I think he was trying to hit as many people as he could." [319]

Doug Quesnel, 22, said “Nothing seemed...wrong until the shots went off.” [320]

EXIT

Harold Ng, 21, said the danger didn’t register even after the firing began. It wasn't until the other students in the class began to run in a panic that Ng began to run. While running, he was shot in the back of the head. "I just swiped the back of my head with my hand, and then when I looked at my hand it was all bloody, Ng said." He ran to a nearby hall.[321]

When the shooting began, chaos erupted. Students dropped to the floor and began crawling, running, and shoving their way to the auditorium doors.[322]

John Giovanni crouched down and bolted for the doors, thinking to himself that a moving target would be more difficult to hit. "I was pushing through people," he said. "You need to get out. You never know how good of a marksman he is. . . My goal was getting out there and running as far as I could to be safe." [323]

Senior Desiree Smith said, “I dropped to the ground under my seat, and could see another girl down there. We just stared at each other. I grabbed her leg and was squeezing it for about five seconds. Then we moved all of a sudden. Everyone was army-crawling toward the back of the auditorium on the floor. As soon as I reached the door, I got halfway hunched over, and then started to run as soon as I got outside."[324]

Freshman Jillian Martinez said, "I ran out of there as fast as I could... Everyone started rushing for doors. Everybody fell over everybody."[325]

NIU Police Chief Donald Grady said students were running through any door they could find in order to get out.[326]

CONCEALMENT

Students who didn't run attempted to hide under their seats or under desks, according to freshman Loren Weese, 18, who was seated on the aisle about halfway up the auditorium. "A lot of people fell," she said. "I don't know if they did that on purpose to avoid being shot." [327]

OTHER

Ducked

Class instructor Joseph Peterson was standing on a stage at the front of the auditorium when the gunman burst in and started shooting. Peterson ducked and was shot in the arm.[328]

Case #47 – Atlantis Plastics	
Synopsis	25-year-old Wesley Higdon shot and killed five co-workers and critically injured another before taking his own life.
Type of Establishment	Workplace
Environment	Indoors
Motive	Retaliation
Number killed	5
Number killed and injured	6
Date of murders	June 25, 2008
Weapons	Hi-Point .45 caliber semi-automatic pistol
Location	Henderson, Kentucky
Shooter status	Committed suicide the same day by shooting himself.

Overview

Wesley Neal Higdon had been employed as a machine operator by the Atlantis Plastics Company in Henderson, Kentucky, for eight months. He had a reputation for being difficult. Higdon was reprimanded by his supervisor Kevin Taylor for spending too much time on his cell phone and for not wearing his safety glasses.

During a work break, Higdon and another employee, Joshua Hinojosa, were across the street at a convenience store and got into an altercation. When Higdon returned to his job, he was reprimanded by Taylor for what had just happened. The supervisor walked him outside, apparently to make him leave the job site. Once outside, Higdon shot Taylor in the head. He then entered the building, walked into the break room, and without saying anything, started shooting. Four people were struck and three died. He went into the plant area, walked up behind Hinojosa, and shot him in the head. He then committed suicide.[329]

COVER

Surveillance video showed that the shootings in the break room seemed to be indiscriminate. Employees could be seen trying to take cover under chairs and tables.[330]

Case #48 – Pinelake Health & Rehab Center

Synopsis	Robert Stewart, 45, opened fire at a nursing home where his estranged wife worked, then was shot and arrested by a police officer.
Type of Establishment	Nursing home
Environment	Outdoors to indoors
Motive	Domestic
Number killed	8
Number killed and injured	10
Date of murders	March 29, 2009
Weapons	Handgun; shotgun; .22 caliber rifle
Location	Carthage, North Carolina
Shooter status	Sentenced on September 2, 2011 to 142 years-to-179-1/2 years in prison.

Overview

Robert Stewart and his wife had a rocky relationship that extended over many years. They married as teens and divorced three years later. Both were involved in other marriages before they reunited and married a second time in June 2002, and then separated again. Not long after the last split, Stewart's wife was working as a nursing assistant at the Pinelake Health and Rehab center, a nursing home and care center for patients with Alzheimer's disease.[331]

On March 29, 2009, Stewart, armed with weapons described by one witness as a "deer gun and a shotgun" and dressed in a bib overall, pulled into the parking lot of the nursing home just before 10:00 a.m., where he shot several times at his wife's car, shattering its windows. He also shot at Michael Lee Cotton when he pulled into the parking lot, shattering the car windows and hitting Cotton with a pellet in the left shoulder.[332]

Stewart entered the facility and went down the hall apparently searching for his wife, who had been reassigned to the Alzheimer unit that morning. Upon realizing that his wife wasn't where she usually worked, he headed to the area for Alzheimer's patients, which was secured by passcode-protected doors. As he proceeded through the halls, Stewart fired at residents in their beds or wheelchairs.[333]

Police received the first emergency calls at approximately 10:00 a.m. and the only police officer on duty, Justin Garner, was dispatched to the scene about one minute later. At about 10:05 a.m., Officer Garner entered the building alone and confronted Stewart. After refusing several orders to drop his weapon, Stewart lowered his shotgun and fired a shot at Garner, wounding him three times in the leg. Garner returned fire and hit the gunman in the upper chest and was able to take him into custody.[334]

COVER

Stewart's wife survived the shooting unharmed, hiding in a bathroom in the Alzheimer's ward secured by passcode-protected doors.[335]

CONCEALMENT

After being shot, Michael Cotton ran into the building and warned those inside about the gunman. He ran to his aunt's room. When he heard the gunman enter the building, he hid in a bathroom. "You could hear him coming down the hallway and just shooting randomly, and people hollering and screaming," he said.[336]

OTHER

Tried to protect others

Nurse Jerry Avant was trying to get patients to safety. Stewart cornered the nurse in a hallway and shot him at least two times. Avant later died in surgery.[337]

CASE #49 – AMERICAN CIVIC ASSOCIATION CENTER	
Synopsis	Jiverly Wong,[iv] 41, opened fire at a center for immigrants before committing suicide.
Type of Establishment	Public building
Environment	Indoors
Motive	Revenge
Number killed	13
Number killed and injured	17
Date of murders	April 3, 2009
Weapons	9mm Beretta; .45 caliber Beretta
Location	Binghamton, New York
Shooter status	Committed suicide the same day by shooting himself.

Overview

Jiverly Wong came to the United States from Vietnam with his family when he was young. Even after years in this country, he "felt degraded because of his inability to speak English, and he was upset about that."[338] He was also upset about recently losing a job when the assembly plant where he worked was closed. He was described as an "angry loner who loved guns." A former co-worker used to joke with a friend about how they thought Wong would "come in mad one day and shoot people. He seemed like that kind of guy."[339]

Wong took English classes at the American Civic Association in Binghamton, New York, which helps refugees and immigrants, until dropping out in March of 2009. On April 3 at about 10:30 a.m., Wong barricaded the rear door of the Civic Association with a vehicle and entered the building. He then opened fire on the people inside.[340] Two of the Civic association's receptionists were among the first victims.[341]

[iv] Recently changed his name to Voong

Wong then focused his violence on a classroom just off the main reception areas where an ESL class was being given to students. Everyone who was in that classroom suffered a gunshot wound. Wong began executing victims, taking some hostage. Police arrived within minutes of the 911 calls; it was later revealed that when Wong heard the sirens, he took his own life with one of his guns. In all, Wong fired 99 rounds; 88 from a 9 mm Beretta and 11 from a .45-caliber Beretta.[342]

EXIT/COVER

Some of those present managed to escape to a basement, while more than a dozen hid in a closet.[343]

CONCEALMENT/OTHER

Played dead

Receptionist Shirley DeLucia was one of the first to be shot, being hit in the stomach. She then pretended to be dead and, when the gunman moved on, hid under a desk and called 911. She stayed on the line for 39 minutes and relayed information until she was rescued.[344]

OTHER

Protected others

Vietnamese immigrant Long Huynh attempted to shield his wife. "I pushed her to the ground and covered her with my body," he said. One bullet passed through him and killed his wife.[345]

Case #50 – Fort Hood Army Base	
Synopsis	Army psychiatrist Nidal Malik Hasan, 39, opened fire on an Army base. Hasan was injured during the attack and later arrested.
Historical note	The Fort Hood attack was the deadliest terrorist attack on a U.S. military base.
Type of Establishment	U.S. Army base
Environment	Indoors
Motive	Terrorism
Number killed	13
Number killed and injured	45
Date of murders	November 5, 2009
Weapons	FN Five-seven semi-automatic pistol; .357 magnum revolver
Location	Fort Hood, Texas
Shooter status	In August 2013, convicted on all charges and sentenced to death. At time of publication, held on military death row.[346]

Overview

Nidal Malik Hasan was born in Virginia to parents who had emigrated from Jordan to the U.S. Hasan joined the U.S. Army, rose to the rank of Major, and worked as a psychiatrist stationed at Ft. Hood in Texas. He worked at the Soldier Readiness Center, where personnel receive routine treatment immediately prior to and returning from deployment.

Hasan reported to family that he felt that as a Muslim committed to his prayers he was discriminated against and not treated with the respect due an officer.[347] He was also distressed over his planned deployment to the Middle East, especially after counseling soldiers who had returned from there suffering post-traumatic stress disorder.

At least six months before November 2009, Hasan had come to the attention of federal authorities due to Internet postings he had apparently made discussing suicide bombings and other threats. He had also been vocal about his concern that the U.S. war on terrorism was a war against Islam.[348]

In the early afternoon of November 5, 2009, Hasan entered the Soldier Readiness Center. According to eyewitnesses, he sat at an empty table, bowed his head for several seconds, then stood up and shouted "*Allahu Akbar*!" before opening fire on defenseless soldiers sitting in a waiting area, then hunting down wounded soldiers in an attempt to finish them off. Many of the wounded soldiers were shot multiple times while they lay on the floor.[349]

Base civilian police Sergeant Kimberly Munley arrived on the scene in response to the report of an emergency at the center. She encountered Hasan leaving the building as he pursued a wounded soldier. Munley and Hasan exchanged gunfire; Munley was hit three times, in the leg and in the wrist, and fell to the ground. In the meantime, civilian police officer Sergeant Mark Todd arrived and fired at the gunman. Hasan was finally felled by shots from Todd and Munley. Todd approached the gunman and kicked a pistol out of his hand. Hasan was placed in handcuffs as he fell unconscious. The incident lasted about 10 minutes.[350]

In a 2011 special report, the Homeland Security and Government Affairs Committee charged that the FBI should have recognized that Hasan had become an adherent of “violent Islamist extremism” before he went on the rampage.[351]

EXIT/COVER

Civilian police officer Sgt. Mark Todd stated that Hasan was firing at people as they were trying to run and hide.[352]

ENGAGE

Unarmed army reserve Capt. John Gaffaney tried to stop Hasan but was mortally wounded in the process.[353]

Witnesses reported that civilian physician assistant Michael Cahill tried to charge Hasan with a chair before being shot and killed.[354]

OTHER

Helped others

As the shooting continued outside, nurses and medics entered the building, secured the doors with a belt, and began helping the wounded.[355]

Case Studies - 2010s

Case #51 – Hartford Beer Distributorship

Synopsis	Omar S. Thornton, 34, facing disciplinary issues, opened fire in his workplace, then committed suicide.
Type of Establishment	Workplace
Environment	Indoors
Motive	Revenge
Number killed	8
Number killed and injured	10
Date of murders	August 3, 2010
Weapons	15-shot Ruger SR9 pistol
Location	Manchester, Connecticut
Shooter status	Committed suicide the same day by shooting himself.

Overview

Omar S. Thornton worked for the Harford Distributors in Manchester, Connecticut. Thornton, who was black, told his girlfriend that he had problems with coworkers who were racist, and that his grievances were not addressed.

Thornton had been recorded on surveillance video in the warehouse stealing beer. On August 3, 2010, he was called in to a disciplinary hearing, and was given the options of being fired or of resigning. He did not argue or protest, but agreed to resign. Then he pulled a Ruger SR9 handgun from what appeared to be a lunch bag, and began firing as he ran through the warehouse.[356] Within moments, he had killed eight workers, and seriously injured two others.

Police responded and began clearing the building. In a final phone call to his mother, Thornton told her he had shot "the five racists." Shortly afterward, he put the gun to his head and killed himself.[357]

Case #52 – Rep. Gabrielle Giffords Public Meeting	
Synopsis	Jared Loughner, 22, opened fire during an outdoor constituent meeting with U.S. Representative Gabrielle Giffords before he was subdued by bystanders and arrested.
Type of Establishment	Shopping center parking lot
Environment	Outdoors
Motive	Political
Number killed	6
Number killed and injured	19
Date of murders	January 8, 2011
Weapon	9mm Glock 19 semi-automatic pistol
Location	Tucson, Arizona
Shooter status	On November 8, 2012, sentenced to serve seven consecutive life terms plus 140 years in prison, without parole.

Overview

Jared Lee Loughner, who dropped out of high school in 2006, was fired from his job at a restaurant, with his manager saying he had undergone a personality transformation. After this, Loughner briefly volunteered at a local animal shelter, walking dogs, but he was asked not to return due to a "failure to follow instructions."

A close friend reported that after Loughner's girlfriend broke up with him, he began to use marijuana and other drugs. He attempted to enlist in the U.S. Army, but was rejected as "unqualified" for service in 2008, in part due to his admission of repeated marijuana use during the application process.

While enrolled in Pima Community College in 2010, Loughner had several run-ins with college police for classroom and library disruptions and was told that he needed to resolve his code of conduct violations and obtain a mental health clearance before being readmitted to the school.

According to a former friend, Loughner had a longstanding dislike for U.S. Representative Gabrielle Giffords, and had often expressed a view that women should not hold positions of power. He repeatedly derided Giffords as a "fake." He attended a rally she held in August 2007, and was upset that she did not (in his view) adequately answer his question "What is government if words have no meaning?"[358]

On the morning of January 8, 2011, Loughner took a taxi to a Safeway supermarket in Casas Adobes, where Rep. Giffords was holding a constituents' meeting in the parking lot. About 20 to 30 people were gathered around a table outside the store. At 10:10 a.m., Loughner opened fire on Giffords (the apparent target) as well as numerous bystanders, killing six people, one of whom was Chief U.S. District Judge John Roll.[359] Thirteen other people were injured by gunfire. Giffords was shot in the head and left in critical condition. Loughner proceeded to fire apparently randomly at other members of the crowd, before being subdued by bystanders and arrested by police.[360]

ENGAGE

Multiple individuals tackled gunman

Loughner apparently stopped to reload but dropped the magazine from his pocket to the sidewalk, and bystander Patricia Maisch grabbed it. Another bystander hit Loughner in the back of the head with a folding chair. The gunman was then tackled to the ground by 74-year-old retired U.S. Army Colonel Bill Badger (who himself had been shot), aided by Maisch and two bystanders.[361]

OTHER

Helped others

While waiting for help to arrive, Giffords' intern Daniel Hernandez, Jr. applied pressure to the gunshot wound to her head and made sure that she did not choke on her blood. Hernandez was credited with saving Giffords' life.[362]

Doctor David Bowman and his wife Nancy, a nurse, who were shopping in the store, immediately set up triage and attended to nine-year-old Christina-Taylor Green, who died from her injury.[363]

Case #53 – IHOP Restaurant

Synopsis	Eduardo Sencion, 32, opened fire at an International House of Pancakes restaurant and later died from a self-inflicted gunshot wound.
Type of Establishment	Restaurant
Environment	Outdoors to indoors to outdoors
Motive	Unknown
Number killed	4
Number killed and injured	11
Date of murders	September 6, 2011
Weapon	Variant of AK-47 assault rifle
Location	Carson City, Nevada
Shooter status	Shot himself immediately afterward and died in hospital.

Overview

Eduardo Sencion, born in Mexico and having a valid U.S. passport worked at a family business in South Lake Tahoe. He filed for bankruptcy protection in January 2009, listing more than $42,000 in outstanding debts for a car, several credit cards and some medical expenses. The case was discharged four months later.[364]

Just before 9:00 a.m. on September 6, 2011, Sencion pulled into the parking lot of an International House of Pancakes restaurant in Carson City, Nevada. Stepping out of his minivan, he opened fire at a woman near a motorcycle, then entered the restaurant and went to a table of uniformed National Guard members, shooting each of them, three of whom were fatally wounded.[365] He then shot and killed another patron.

Sencion then walked back to the parking lot and began firing into other businesses in the strip mall. He then shot himself in the head and was pronounced dead later at a local hospital.[366]

Case #54 – Salon Meritage	
Synopsis	Scott Evans Dekraii, 42, opened fire inside a hair salon, killing eight.
Type of Establishment	Business
Environment	Indoors to outdoors
Motive	Domestic
Number killed	8
Number killed and injured	9
Date of murders	October 12, 2011
Weapons	9mm Springfield; Smith & Wesson .44 magnum; Heckler & Hoch .45
Location	Seal Beach, California
Shooter status	Convicted in 2014 of multiple counts of murder and imprisoned.[367]

Overview

Scott Evans Dekraii had lost a court case with his ex-wife Michelle involving their seven-year-old son. Michelle had claimed in court filings that her ex-husband was unstable and physically abused her during their marriage. Dekraii threatened violence.

At shortly after 1:00 p.m. on October 12, 2011, he drove to the Salon Meritage, where Michelle worked as a hairstylist, and opened fire on stylists and customers inside the shop, killing his ex-wife and six others. The shooting lasted approximately two minutes.[368]

Dekraii left the salon and headed to his vehicle. On the way, he encountered David Caouette, 64, who had been visiting the restaurant next door to the salon. Dekraii fired through the front windshield and passenger window of the vehicle, killing Caouette.[369]

Dekraii was arrested and surrendered without incident after being stopped about one-half mile from the scene of the crime. He told police he had multiple weapons in his car.[370]

EXIT/COVER

Some of those inside the salon tried to escape by running into the street, locking themselves in private treatment rooms, or hiding in neighboring businesses.[371]

COVER

One employee who locked herself in one of the salon's rooms was unharmed. A man who locked himself in a bathroom was wounded.[372]

Salon co-owner Sandy Fannin survived unharmed by hiding at the back of the property. Kimberly Criswell, owner of a nail salon two doors away, said she and her customers heard gunshots. Her receptionist saw through the window as a man in the parking lot was shot. Criswell said, "We all ran into the bathroom and locked the door." [373]

OTHER

Pleaded for life

Randy Fannin, the owner of Salon Meritage, was the first person to be shot, and died. He reportedly said to the gunman, "Please don't do this. There's another way. Let's go outside and talk." Dekraii said, "Shut up," and continued firing.[374]

Case #55 - Oikos University	
Synopsis	One L. Goh, 43, a former student, opened fire in a nursing classroom of a Korean Christian college. He fled the scene by car and was later arrested nearby.
Type of Establishment	University
Environment	Indoors
Motive	Revenge
Number killed	7
Number killed and injured	10
Date of murders	April 2, 2012
Weapon	.45 caliber handgun
Location	Oakland, California
Shooter status	Arrested and charged with seven counts of murder and three counts of attempted murder. In January 2013 he was deemed unfit for trial due to diagnosis of paranoid schizophrenia and held in a treatment facility in an attempt to render him competent for trial.[375] In July 2017 he was sentenced to seven consecutive life terms in prison.[376]

Overview

In 2009, One Goh had a failed marriage and a failed business. There were several court judgments and tax liens against him dating back to 2006. He owed more than $23,000 in federal taxes at one point and thousands of dollars more to banks and apartment owners. In an attempt to start over, he left Virginia and moved to California where his father lived.[377]

Goh enrolled in the nursing program at Oikos College, a Korean Christian college in Oakland. At 43, Goh felt bullied and disrespected by his much-younger classmates, saying they made fun of his English-speaking skills.[378] Not long into the program, he dropped out and tangled with the administration in an effort to get back his $6,000 tuition.

On the morning of April 2, 2012, Goh arrived on campus with a .45 caliber handgun looking for a particular administrator. When he discovered that she was not in the building, he went into a classroom and told the students to stand up and line up against the wall. Then, when they would not all cooperate with his instructions, he opened fire.[379]

Goh fled the scene in a car belonging to one of the victims. He drove to a mall in Alameda, about five miles from the school, and told a security guard that he needed to speak to police because he had shot several people. He did not resist when taken into custody.[380]

EXIT

Brian Snow was at a nearby credit union when he first heard the shots and saw a victim run out of the building.[381]

Dawinder Kaar was shot in the arm as she stopped to help a friend who had fallen on the classroom floor; then she ran outside.[382]

Case #56 – Cafe Racer

Synopsis	Ian Stawicki, 40, gunned down four patrons at a café, and another person during a carjacking nearby, then shot himself as police closed in.
Type of Establishment	Restaurant
Environment	Indoors to outdoors
Motive	Retaliation
Number killed	5
Number killed and injured	7
Date of murders	May 30, 2012
Weapon	.45 caliber semi-automatic handgun
Location	Seattle, Washington
Shooter status	Committed suicide the same day by shooting himself.

Overview

On May 30, 2012, Ian Stawicki's girlfriend thought he was acting "kind of crazy" and she would not let him have the car.[383] He apparently took his mother's car and went to the Café Racer in the University District of Seattle. Stawicki had been banned from the café for disruptive behavior, but came in anyway and attempted to place an order. After the barista declined to serve him, he opened fire with two .45 caliber handguns, killing four customers and wounding the café's chef.[384]

About a half-hour after the cafe shootings, Stawicki fatally shot Gloria Leonidas in a parking lot, and then fled in her car. Later that afternoon, as police closed in on him, Stawicki knelt on a sidewalk in West Seattle and shot himself in the head.[385]

CONCEALMENT

People scrambled for cover as soon as Stawicki began shooting. One man calling 911 from Cafe Racer said, “Someone came in and shot a bunch of people. I'm hiding in the bathroom. We need help right away.” [386]

ENGAGE/EXIT

As the gunman aimed at him, one customer grabbed bar stools and threw them at Stawicki. The tactic created enough of a delay in the shooting that a few other customers were able to escape through the door which the gunman had blocked.[387]

"My brother died in the World Trade Center," the man later told police, who provided an account of the interview. After his brother's death, he said, he resolved that if something like this ever happened, I would never hide under a table." [388]

ENGAGE

Gloria Leonidas had just dropped off a friend in a parking lot when she was confronted by Stawicki. The gunman started beating her. Police said that she knocked the gun from his hand before he fatally shot her in the head. He then took off in her car.[389]

OTHER

Bystanders helped

Even while Stawicki was still in the parking lot, a couple rushed across the street and began to administer CPR to Leonidas.[390]

Case #57 – Cinemark Movie Theater	
Synopsis	James Holmes, 24, opened fire in a movie theater during the opening night of a movie, and was later arrested outside.
Type of Establishment	Movie theater
Environment	Indoors
Motive	Unknown
Number killed	12
Number killed and injured	70
Date of murders	July 20, 2012
Weapon	Smith & Wesson M&P15 rifle; Remington 870 Express tactical shotgun; two Glock .22 handguns
Location	Aurora, Colorado
Shooter status	Holmes was convicted and in August 2015 received 12 life sentences plus 3,318 years.[391]

Overview

James Holmes was a graduate student at the University of Colorado Denver/Anschutz Medical Campus but was in the process of withdrawing from the graduate program in neuroscience.[392]

On July 20, 2012, Holmes bought a ticket to the midnight screening of the new Batman movie, *The Dark Knight Rises*, at the Cinemark movie theater in Aurora, Colorado, and sat on the front row of the theater. About 20 minutes into the film, he left through an emergency exit door, which he propped open. He apparently then went to his car parked near the exit door, changed into body armor and donned a gas mask, and reentered the theater through the propped-open door.[393]

Other audience members did not at first suspect anything dangerous, thinking it was just someone dressed in costume for the movie or part of a special event tied to the movie premiere.[394]

Holmes set off a canister of gas and opened fire with a variety of weapons. He fired a shotgun at the ceiling and then at the audience. He also fired a semi-automatic rifle with 100-round drum magazine, which apparently malfunctioned after he began firing. Finally, Holmes fired a Glock 22 40-caliber handgun. He shot toward the back of the auditorium, then toward people in the aisles. One bullet passed through a wall and hit a person in the next theater.[395]

Police arrived within 90 seconds of the first phone calls to emergency services at 12:39. About 12:45 a.m., police apprehended Holmes behind the cinema, next to his car, without resistance.[396] His rampage had resulted in 12 dead and another 58 wounded.

EXIT

Moviegoers fell to the floor and crawled over each other in an effort to get out. Some dragged bloodied bodies to the lobby.[397]

The man next to moviegoer Chris Ramos had already been shot, and others were falling. Ramos jammed his head down toward the floor and grabbed for his sister at the same time. "People were jumping over seats, jumping over you," Ramos said. On the floor, they felt bodies; as they crawled they came across a man with a bleeding leg wound. Ramos and his sister dragged the man as far as they could, and were eventually met in the lobby by police officers.[398]

Jennifer Seeger was sitting in the second row of the theater when the gunman burst in. He pointed a rifle at her face. She dove into the aisle and tucked herself under a chair, and Holmes shot a person behind her. "I had bullets that were on my forehead, burning my forehead, and I told myself, I need to get out of here...I crawled on the ground and I just laid in a ball and waited for him to go up the stairs," Seeger said, then told her friend that they had to leave. "At that point, I was trying to crawl out but then everybody was crawling back in and saying, 'Don't go over there. He's going to shoot everybody trying to get out of the main doors,' and he was. All I hear is gunshot after gunshot." [399]

Spenser Sherman recalled, "Everybody had dropped to the floor after the first couple gunshots, and then he fired some more. And then after that, there was a pause in the gunshots. But at that point, my boyfriend was like 'This is the time, we need to go, and we need to get out of the theater right now.' So we ran." [400]

When the gunman tossed a smoke canister, Jordan Crofter ran for his life and was the first to make it to the lobby.[401]

Resharee Goodlo said, "I ran. I pushed. I did whatever I had to do to get out." [402]

OTHER

Played dead

"I heard the gunshots...and I fell to the floor, crawling on the ground to try to get out," said moviegoer Corbin Dates said. As the gunman walked along the left side of the theater, Dates crawled up the right side, urging others to pretend that they were dead. He made it out, but saw bodies slumped over in their movie seats as he fled.[403]

Chandler Brannon saw a smoke bomb go off and heard what sounded like fireworks. He then realized that the noises he was hearing were gunshots. "I told my girlfriend to just play dead," he said." [404]

Case #58 – Sikh Temple	
Synopsis	Wade Michael Page, 40, a white supremacist, opened fire in the parking lot of a Sikh temple, then went inside and shot congregants gathered prior to a service. He killed himself in the parking lot after being shot by a police officer.
Type of Establishment	Temple
Environment	Indoors
Motive	Domestic terrorism[405]
Number killed	6
Number killed and injured	9
Date of murders	August 5, 2012
Weapon	9mm semi-automatic handgun equipped with 19-round large capacity magazine
Location	Oak Creek, Wisconsin
Shooter status	Committed suicide after being shot by police at the scene.

Overview

Wade Michael Page was a U.S. Army veteran who others described as a “frustrated neo-Nazi.” He had participated in several white supremacist rock bands, and had drawn the attention of groups that monitor extremist activity.[406]

On August 5, 2012, Page went to the Sikh temple in Oak Creek, Wisconsin and began shooting. He shot two people in the parking lot, then went inside the temple and continued to fire on people who were gathered to prepare for the Sunday service.

Page ambushed and opened fire on a veteran police officer who responded to the emergency and was attending to a victim on scene; the officer survived.[407]

Page killed himself in the parking lot after being shot by another police officer.[408]

CONCEALMENT

Several children saw the gunman firing and alerted women who were cooking a meal for the service. Some hid in a pantry and were unharmed.[409]

Case #59 – Accent Signage Systems, Inc.	
Synopsis	Andrew Engeldinger, 36, opened fire on employees at his workplace and then committed suicide.
Type of Establishment	Business
Environment	Indoors
Motive	Revenge
Number killed	6
Number killed and injured	8
Date of murders	September 27, 2012
Weapons	Glock 9mm handgun
Location	Minneapolis, Minnesota
Shooter status	Committed suicide the same day by shooting himself.

Overview

Andrew Engeldinger was a longtime employee of Accent Signage Systems in Minneapolis who had clashed with superiors over poor performance and chronic tardiness. He had struggled with paranoia and delusions and had withdrawn from his family. In September, 2012, Engeldinger had received a letter of reprimand which warned of possible termination.

On September 27, he was asked to meet in the office of Operations Director John Souter. Engeldinger went to his car and returned with a Glock 9mm handgun. In the meeting, he was fired and was given his final paycheck. He pulled out the gun, and a struggle ensued between him, Souter, and employee Rami Cooks. Souter and Cooks were wounded, and Cooks died.

Engeldinger reloaded and left Souter's office. Encountering company owner Reuven Rahamin, he fatally shot him and went into the sales staff area. He shot and killed employee Jacob Beneke, then went to the loading dock area. There he shot employee Ron Edberg, as well as UPS driver Keith Basinki, who was in his truck at the dock area; both men died.

Engeldinger then went to the company's production area where he shot and wounded employee Eric River, who later died. Another employee was grazed by a bullet. Engeldinger then went to the basement and shot himself in the head.[410]

ENGAGE

Souter opened his office door to see Engeldinger raising a gun. Souter grabbed the barrel and pointed it upward as the gunman began firing. Souter was hit twice and fell.[411]

CASE #60 – SANDY HOOK ELEMENTARY SCHOOL	
Synopsis	Adam Peter Lanza, 20, fatally shot 20 children and 6 adults before killing himself at Sandy Hook Elementary School. Before driving to the school, he had shot and killed his mother.
Historical note	The Sandy Hook massacre was the 2nd deadliest school shooting in U.S. history.
Type of Establishment	School
Environment	Indoors
Motive	Unknown
Number killed	27
Number killed and injured	29
Date of murders	December 14, 2012
Weapons	.22-caliber rifle; Bushmaster .223-caliber semi-automatic assault rifle equipped with 30-round large capacity ammunition magazine.[v] [412]
Location	Newtown, Connecticut
Shooter status	Committed suicide the same day by shooting himself.

Overview

Adam Peter Lanza lived with his mother in Newtown, Connecticut. He was a recluse who liked to play violent video games.[413] Sometime before 9:30 a.m. on December 14, 2012, Lanza shot his mother in the

---

[v] According to the Danbury State's Attorney, police also recovered in Lanza's possession a 9mm handgun and three loaded 30-round large-capacity ammunition magazines for the Bushmaster. Six additional 30-round large-capacity ammunition magazines were recovered at the scene. A loaded unknown make 12-gauge shotgun was found in Lanza's car. All of the guns used in the shooting were purchased by Lanza's mother.

head multiple times at their home, and then headed to Sandy Hook Elementary School which he had attended as a child.[414]

Wearing black military-style gear, including a bulletproof vest and mask, and using his mother's Bushmaster XM-15 rifle, Lanza shot his way through a locked glass door at the front of the school and started shooting, continuing for 15 to 20 minutes and firing between 50 and 100 rounds. He shot all of his victims multiple times, mostly in two first-grade classrooms, killing 14 children in one room and six in the other. The student victims were eight boys and 12 girls, between six and seven years of age, and the six adults were all women who worked at the school. Lanza shot himself in the head as first responders arrived.[415]

Investigators later found weapons at the Lanza home including a 7-foot pole with a blade on one side and a spear on another; a metal bayonet; three samurai swords; a .323-caliber bolt-action rifle; a .22 caliber Savage Mark II rifle; and a .22 caliber Volcanic starter pistol. Literature removed from the house included a news article on the 2008 shooting at Northern Illinois University and a National Rifle Association guide to pistol shooting.[416]

COVER

A teacher and students took refuge in a gymnasium closet.[417]

First grade teacher Kaitlin Roig hid 14 students in a bathroom and barricaded the door, telling them to be completely quiet to remain safe.[418]

School library staff Yvonne Cech and Maryann Jacob tried to hide 18 children in an area of the library which was used for lockdown in practice drills, but on discovering that one of the doors would not lock, they had the children crawl into a storage room. Cech barricaded the door with a filing cabinet.[419]

Music teacher Maryrose Kristopik barricaded her fourth-grader students in a small supply closet. Lanza arrived moments later, pounding and yelling "Let me in," while the students in Kristopik's class quietly hid inside.[420]

Two third graders, chosen as classroom helpers, were walking down the hallway to the office to deliver the morning attendance sheet during the shooting. Teacher Abbey Clements pulled both children into her classroom, where they hid. They were unharmed.[421]

Reading specialist Laura Feinstein grabbed two students from outside her classroom and hid with them under desks after they heard gunshots. Feinstein called the school office and attempted to call 9-1-1 but was unable to connect because her cell phone did not have reception. She hid with the children for approximately 40 minutes, before law enforcement came to lead them out of the room.[422]

CONCEALMENT/OTHER

Tried to protect others

Teacher Victoria Soto attempted to hide several children in a closet and cupboards. As Lanza entered her classroom, Soto reportedly told him that the children were in the auditorium. Several of the children then came out of their hiding place and tried to run for safety and were shot dead. Soto got between the students and Lanza, who then fatally shot her. {After the shooting, six surviving children from Soto's class crawled out of the cupboards and fled the school. As reported by his parents, a 6-year-old boy in Ms. Soto's class fled with a group of his classmates and the children escaped through the door when the gunman shot their teacher.} [423]

CONCEALMENT

School nurse Sarah Cox hid under a desk in her office, and saw Lanza enter her office and stand 20 feet away before turning around and leaving. Cox and school secretary Barbara Halstead then hid in a first-aid supply closet for up to four hours, after calling 9-1-1.[424]

ENGAGE

Confronted gunman

School principal Dawn Hochsprung and school psychologist Mary Sherlach were meeting with other faculty members when they heard gunshots outside. Hochsprung and Sherlach left the room and rushed toward the sounds and encountered Lanza, who shot both women dead as they confronted him.[425]

OTHER
Alerted others

A custodian ran through hallways, alerting classrooms.[426]

OTHER
Tried to protect others

Teacher Natalie Hammond was in a faculty meeting when gunshots were heard. She pressed her body against the door to keep it closed. Lanza shot through the door, hitting Hammond in the leg and arm.[427]

Teacher's aide Anne Marie Murphy shielded a 6-year-old boy with her body; the bullets killed them both.[428]

Paraprofessional Rachel D'Avino, who had been employed at the school for just over a week, also died trying to protect her students.[429]

OTHER
Played dead

First-grade substitute teacher Lauren Rousseau was shot in the face and killed. All but one of the children in her classroom were shot dead. The sole survivor, a six-year-old girl, played dead and remained still until the building was quiet and she thought it was safe to leave. Covered in blood, she was the first child to escape the building.[430]

CASE #61 – SANTA MONICA CITY AND COLLEGE

Synopsis	John Zawahri, 23, killed his father and brother and set fire to his father's home. He then hijacked a car and headed to Santa Monica College, firing at a city bus and at cars, injuring several persons. Arriving at campus, he fired on more individuals, and was finally killed by police in the college library.
Type of Establishment	College campus
Environment	Indoors and outdoors
Motive	Unknown
Number killed	5
Number killed and injured	9
Date of murders	June 7, 2013
Weapons	.223 caliber assault rifle; .44 caliber "black powder" revolver; three "zip" guns
Location	Santa Monica, California
Shooter status	Killed by police

Overview

Some who knew him said that 23-year-old John Zawahri had struggled with his parents' marital problems, and had a history of mental issues. [431] A teacher saw Zawahri looking online at assault weapons. A high school classmate reported that Zawahri had showed him a samurai sword and talked about students at school whom he wanted to hurt. Zawahri was admitted to a psychiatric hospital but did not stay for long.[432]

On the morning of June 7, 2013, Zawahri killed his father and brother at his father's home, and set fire to the house. Leaving the house, he fired upon Debra Fine who was driving home. "He looked right at me," she said. "Stared right at me and then shot. No hesitation." Fine recovered from her wounds.[433]

The gunman then hijacked a car and forced the driver to go to Santa Monica College. On the way, he fired at a city bus, resulting in three people being injured, and on cars in the area, including a patrol car.

Carlo Franco and daughter Marcela were on their way to buy school books. They were the first victims after Zawahri arrived on campus. He sprayed their SUV with gunfire. Franco was killed instantly; his daughter died at a hospital two days later. Margarita Gomez, 68, was shot outside the school library, and died instantly.[434] The gunman then proceeded to the college library, where he was confronted by police and shot dead.

The shooter wore dark black clothing and a tactical vest. Police recovered a .223 caliber assault rifle bearing no serial number, and .223 magazines capable of holding 30 rounds (illegal to possess in California). A .44 caliber "black powder" revolver had been converted to fire .45 caliber rounds. Detectives also recovered three "zip" guns, apparently handmade.[435]

EXIT/CONCEALMENT

Students in the library dived for cover or ran for safety as police exchanged gunfire with Zawahri.[436]

Sam Luster heard gunfire. He saw students at the entrance of the library running down toward the bottom of the library. He hid under a desk before heading to the exit.[437]

Student Priscilla Morales and her friends looked out a library window and saw people running. They grabbed their things and started to leave, but as they opened the door they heard gunshots. So they closed the door and hid.[438]

Police Chief Jacqueline Seabrooks said that some students hid in a "safe room" in the library and barricaded the door. "They stacked items found in the safe room against the door, hunkered down and avoided shots fired through the drywall at them while they were in that room," she said.[439]

OTHER

Played dead

Debra Fine was the first person shot after Zawahri left his father's home. As she fell to her side and pretended to be dead, she called her husband for help.[440]

Case #62 – Todel Apartments	
Synopsis	Pedro Alberto Vargas, 42, shot his apartment building's managers, began firing into the street, then went to another apartment in the building and killed three occupants. He took two hostages in another apartment before police finally killed him and rescued the hostages.
Type of Establishment	Apartment building
Environment	Indoors and outdoors
Motive	Unknown
Number killed	6
Number killed and injured	6
Date of murders	July 26, 2013
Weapon	9 mm Glock handgun
Location	Hialeah, Florida
Shooter status	Killed by police

Overview

Pedro Alberto Vargas was known as a dedicated son and talented graphic designer. He lived with and cared for his mother in an apartment in Hialeah, Florida. He had earned a technical education degree, and in 2004 began work at Miami Dade College in media services. His work performance evaluations had been positive, but later a supervisor noted that he lacked social skills and found it hard to accept change.

After four years at MDC, Vargas was forced to resign when it was learned that he had downloaded inappropriate files off the Internet. After his resignation, two former supervisors received anonymous threats via email, texts and Facebook. Vargas' next job lasted only three months before he was fired. Co-workers from that firm also received anonymous emails. The pattern was repeated at another company where Vargas worked until he was let go.[441] He later admitted having been the author of the messages.

On July 26, 2013, Vargas called 911 to report that someone was following him and that he was the victim of sorcery. Two police officers were dispatched to his apartment but left after learning from his mother that he had gone to buy gasoline. When Vargas returned home, he was carrying a container of gasoline and a bag of cash. At about 6:30 p.m., he set fire to the money. When smoke from the fire apparently caused the building's husband and wife managers, Italo and Samira Pisciotti, to investigate, Vargas shot and killed them.[442]

Police arrived within minutes. Vargas shot at them from the balcony but missed. He fired 10 to 20 shots into the street, killing 33-year-old Carlos Gavilanes as he got out of his car.[443] Vargas then went to Apt. 304, kicked in the door, and shot and killed 64-year-old Patricio Simono; his wife, 51-year-old Merly Niebles; and their daughter Priscilla Perez.

Going to another apartment, Vargas then took two hostages. Police tried to negotiate with him for several hours before the SWAT team entered and killed Vargas and rescued the hostages.[444]

When he was killed, Vargas had two full magazines of ammunition. Hialeah police said that the weapon used was a 9-mm Glock handgun purchased legally in 2010.[445]

CONCEALMENT

Priscilla Perez was hiding in the bathtub when she was shot and killed.[446]

OTHER

Pleaded for their lives

Zoeb and Sarrida Nek pleaded for their lives, weeping on their knees in their apartment as Vargas pointed a gun at their heads.[447] They were rescued.

Case #63 – Washington Navy Yard	
Synopsis	Defense subcontractor employee Aaron Alexis opened fire in Building 197 of the Washington Navy Yard, killing 12 and injuring 14. After an hour-long rampage, Alexis was killed by a DC officer.
Type of Establishment	Military complex
Environment	Indoors
Motive	Mental illness
Number killed	12
Number killed and injured	26
Date of murders	September 16, 2013
Weapon	Remington 870 shotgun
Location	Washington, DC
Shooter status	Killed by police

Overview

34-year-old military contractor Aaron Alexis was a computer technician for a defense subcontractor. He had been an enlisted petty officer, discharged from the Navy in 2010 due to what was described as a "pattern of misconduct" which apparently involved insubordination and disorderly conduct, among other things. But with no firm evidence, he was given an honorable discharge.

He started his job as a defense contractor at the Navy Yard just a week before the attacks. He entered the Navy base using a valid identification card.[448]

Two days before the rampage, Alexis had visited a gun range in Virginia, purchasing a Remington shotgun and a small amount of ammunition.[449]

Shortly after 8:00 a.m. on September 16, dressed in black, Alexis went to a fourth floor restroom in Building 197 and emerged with a shotgun. He killed a security guard and took the guard's 9mm handgun, then began firing on the fourth floor. He apparently fired at random, targeting no one in particular. He went to the third floor and then to the lobby, where he dropped the shotgun and began firing the handgun.

The attack put government buildings and eight nearby schools on lockdown. Agents and officers from multiple local and federal law enforcement agencies responded to the scene. As police units engaged him, Alexis went back to a higher floor. He was killed on the third floor by a D.C. officer. The rampage lasted for about an hour. Twelve were dead and 14 more were injured.

In the months before the shooting, Alexis seemed to suffer from increasing paranoia and delusions. An electronic document recovered after the shooting referred to the "ultra-low frequency attack" against him. "To be perfectly honest that is what has driven me to this," it said. His shotgun was etched with the words "My ELF weapon" as well as "End to the Torment!" and "Better off this way."[450]

One month before the attack, Alexis had complained to his employer that people were talking to him through the walls and ceilings of his hotel room and sending microwave vibrations into his body to deprive him of sleep.

EXIT

Cmdr. Tim Jirus was sitting in an office in the Navy Yard, writing an email, when he heard gunfire. When it became clear that there was a gunman on the loose, he and another man tried to help people out of the building. They were standing outside when two shots rang out. "One hit him. The other one – it didn't hit me," said Jirus. "I looked down. The other's guy's dead."[451]

CONCEALMENT

13-year-employee John Weaver watched Alexis methodically shoot six of his friends, killing five of them. "I heard a really loud bang. Two seconds later, I heard another really loud bang and then I realized somebody's in here and they are shooting people...So I popped my head up and I saw him pointing his gun at my friend, and he shot her." Weaver ducked behind his cubicle, pulled a cabinet to block the entrance, and hid beneath his desk as he called 911.[452]

CONCEALMENT

Moments after Alexis fired a blast at them, Bertillia Lavern and her supervisor Andy Kelly were hiding under a desk in a cubicle. "Glass shattered right by my head," Lavern said. "It was on the edge of Andy's cubicle."[453]

Case #64 – Cedarville Rancheria	
Synopsis	Former tribal leader Cherie Lash Rhoades, 44, opened fire at a tribal hearing, killing four and critically wounding two others in an attack with a gun and then a knife. While attacking one victim outside, she was subdued and placed into custody.
Type of Establishment	Indian Reservation
Environment	Outdoors
Motive	Retaliation/Revenge
Number killed	4
Number killed and injured	6
Date of murders	February 20, 2014
Weapon	9mm handguns
Location	Alturas, California
Shooter status	Charged with four counts of murder and two of attempted murder; sentenced to death in 2017.[454]

Overview

Cherie Lash Rhoades, former leader of her Paiute Indian tribe's Cedarville Rancheria, was accused of stealing money from the tribe, most of whom are relatives. She was summoned to a tribal hearing on February 20, 2014. At the hearing, led by her brother, tribal chairman Rurik Davis, Rhoades pulled out a gun and opened fire. Four people were killed, including her brother, 19-year-old niece, 30-year-old nephew and the tribal administrator. Two others were hospitalized in serious condition.[455]

When Rhoades ran out of ammunition she continued her attack with a butcher knife she grabbed from the kitchen.

The Modoc County Undersheriff said that he was the first on scene at the tribal office, minutes after the shooting. When he arrived, Rhoades was in the parking lot, stabbing one of the victims in the chest. Rhoades fumbled and dropped the knife, and the officer tackled her. The entire attack was captured on camera from surveillance mounted outside the tribal office, inside the office, and on the officer's body camera.[456]

When Alturas Police Chief Ken Barnes arrived at the scene, he found an empty handgun and 16 shell casings, and a second handgun had eight rounds in it. He testified that he believed the gun had jammed, preventing Rhoades from killing more people.[457]

EXIT

Rhoades attacked suddenly during the hearing. There was not much chance for anyone to escape, but Nikki Munholland, financial assistant for the tribe, ran out of the room after the first shot and survived.[458]

CASE #65 – ISLA VISTA COMMUNITY	
Synopsis	Elliot Rodger, 22, stabbed three men to death in his apartment; drove to a sorority house and shot three female students; drove to a nearby deli and shot and killed a male student; sped through the city, shooting and wounding several pedestrians and hitting others with his car; exchanged gunfire with police; then killed himself inside his car.
Type of Establishment	Multiple locations
Environment	Indoors/outdoors
Motive	Rage/Racial
Number killed	6
Number killed and injured	20
Date of murders	May 23, 2014
Weapons	Glock 34 handgun; 2 SIG Sauer P226 handguns; two knives
Location	Isla Vista, California
Shooter status	Committed suicide the same day by shooting himself.

Overview

Elliot Rodger wrote in his journal that he fantasized about punishing "all of the popular kids and young couples for the crime of having a better life than me." When he turned 19 in the summer of 2011, he marked it as the start of his "endgame," in which he would either find "love, sex, friends, fun, acceptance, a sense of belonging," or vengeance against those who did enjoy that life.[459]

On May 23, 2014, Rodger killed his two roommates and a friend in his Isla Vista apartment, each with multiple stab wounds. He then drove to a sorority house and knocked on the door. When no one answered, he shot three female students outside, killing two of them and wounding the third. He drove to a nearby deli and fired several gunshots inside, fatally wounding a male student.

He sped through Isla Vista and shot and wounded several pedestrians and struck multiple others with his car. He exchanged gunfire twice with police and received a non-fatal wound. Then Rodger shot and killed himself inside the car. Police investigated a total of 17 crime scenes.[460]

Writings discovered after his death showed a man filled with rage, frustrated over not having a girlfriend, family conflicts, and his contempt for racial minorities and interracial couples. In a video uploaded to YouTube, Rodger said he wanted to punish women for rejecting him and to punish sexually-active men for living a more enjoyable life than his. "All those girls I've desired so much. They have all rejected me and looked down on me as an inferior man if I ever made a sexual advance toward them, while they throw themselves at these obnoxious brutes," he says. "I take great pleasure in slaughtering all of you." Elliot's mental health issues were well known to his family and he had been seeing two therapists prior to his death.

EXIT

Police told student to "go inside and stay inside" as the killer was unleashing a hail of bullets around the campus.

EXIT

Deli goers who were outside fled the area as the shooter killed one of the customers with what was described as "a rain of gunfire."

CONCEALMENT

Student Sierra Swartz was walking down the street when Rodger confronted her with a black pistol and fired it. "I started walking the other way." That walk turned into a run for her life after more shots were fired at her. She ran into the first open door she saw, pleading with the residents, "I just got shot at. I just got shot at. Please, just let me hang out here for a second," she said. The residents locked the doors, turned off all the lights and called 911.[461]

Case #66 – Marysville-Pitchuck High School	
Synopsis	Student Jaylen Fryberg opened fire in the lunchroom at Marysville-Pitchuck High School, killing four students and wounding two others and then killing himself.
Type of Establishment	High School
Environment	Indoors
Motive	Personal/Romance
Number killed	4
Number killed and injured	5
Date of murders	October 24, 2014
Weapon	.40 caliber Beretta handgun
Location	Seattle, Washington
Shooter status	Committed suicide the same day by shooting himself.

Overview

On October 24, 2014 Jaylen Fryberg, a 15-year-old freshman student at Marysville-Pitchuck High School, texted several students and invited them to meet him for lunch. At lunchtime, the invited students were sitting together at one table. Fryberg entered the school cafeteria and sat down at a different table. At 10:39 a.m. he stood up, approached the table where his friends were, and had a verbal altercation with one or more of them. He then pulled out a .40-caliber Beretta handgun and fired at least eight shots, killing four students and then killing himself.

The motive for the shooting was not clear, but Fryberg had made posts on Twitter that suggested a rocky romance and also stated in one that "he was not going to go out alone."

ENGAGE

Although initial reports stated that the shooter killed himself when approached by a teacher, it is unclear if Fryberg ever saw the teacher before he committed suicide.

EXIT/CONCEALMENT

Some of the students began to run. Student Jordan Luton and others hit the ground, some hiding under tables.[462]

ASSESS/EXIT

Student Austin Taylor [said] that he had just finished eating when he saw the shooter. "At first, I thought it was just someone making a really loud noise...like a big loud pop...until I heard four more after. And I saw three kids just fall from the table." Austin said he ducked under a table. When the shooting stopped, he said he looked out and saw the shooter was trying to reload. "When that happened, I just ran in the opposite direction, and I was out of there as fast as I could," he said.[463]

OTHER

Played Dead

Nate Hatch, 14, was shot in the face. He dropped to the ground...lay still on the floor and pretended he was dead as the sound of bullets rang out around him.[464]

Case #67 – Emanuel AME Church	
Synopsis	Dylann Roof, a white man age 21, attended a prayer meeting at the Emanuel AME Church in Charleston and then opened fire, killing the pastor and eight others and wounding one. The gunman fled but was later captured without resistance.
Type of Establishment	Church
Environment	Indoors
Motive	Racial
Number killed	9
Number killed and injured	10
Date of murders	June 17, 2015
Weapon	Glock 41; .45 caliber handgun
Location	Charleston, South Carolina
Shooter status	Arrested and indicted on 33 counts, including federal hate crimes and firearms charges. Sentenced to death in January 2017.[465]

Overview

On the evening of June 17, 2015, after a quarterly conference attended by about 60 at the historic Emanuel African American Methodist Episcopal Church in Charleston, South Carolina, twelve members remained behind to hold a Bible study. Dylann Roof, a white man, entered the room and asked who the minister was. When told that Rev. Clementa Pinckney, 41, was the church's head pastor, Roof sat near him at a round table.

About 9:00 p.m., as the group prepared to share a concluding prayer, Roof stood, pulled out a .45 caliber semi-automatic pistol and said he had come to kill black people. He shot the Rev. Pinckney first, at near point-blank range. Retired minister Daniel Simmons tried to protect the pastor, a father of two young children, but Roof shot him multiple times, too.

All of the dead and dying suffered multiple gunshot wounds. An hour after he arrived, Roof climbed into his car and left.[466]

The killer was able to fire off 77 rounds in a short period of time. He was captured without resistance the next morning at a traffic stop more than 200 miles from the crime scene. He later stated that he committed the shootings in hopes of igniting a race war.

Joseph Meek, Jr., Roof's former best friend, said after the shootings that Roof had begun ranting about the murders of Trayvon Martin and Freddie Gray and saying that black people were "taking over the world" and that "someone needed to do something about it for the white race," Meek said, quoting Roof. "He said he wanted segregation between whites and blacks. I said, 'That's not the way it should be.' But he kept talking about it."[467]

One of the survivors was reportedly a five-year-old girl who obeyed her grandmother's instructions to play dead. Another was Polly Sheppard, whom Roof passed her as she was on her knees praying. He said, "I am going to let you live so you can tell the story of what happened," and told her that he planned to kill himself.

OTHER

Stayed completely still

At the third table from the rear door, Felicia Sanders dropped to the floor and pulled her granddaughter close. "Shhh," she whispered urgently, then willed herself to be still.

OTHER

Locked door

Two others survived, unseen by Roof, locked in the Rev. Pinckney's office: the pastor's wife, Jennifer Pinckney, and one of their young daughters.[468]

Case #68 – Chattanooga Military Facilities

Synopsis	Muhammad Youssef Abdulazeez, 24, attacked two military facilities in succession in a shooting rampage.
Type of Establishment	Military Facilities
Environment	Outdoors
Motive	Terrorism
Number killed	5
Number killed and injured	7
Date of murders	July 16, 2015
Weapon	AK-47, shotgun, 9mm handgun
Location	Chattanooga, TN
Shooter status	Killed by police

Overview

Kuwaiti-born Muhammad Youssef Abdulazeez emigrated to the U.S. with his parents and became a U.S. citizen in 2003. He earned an electrical engineering degree from the University of Tennessee at Chattanooga and learned to manage electrical power systems as an intern for the Tennessee Valley Authority. He worked briefly as an engineer for a nuclear generating station but was let go after failing a drug test. [469] In the three months prior to the shootings, Abdulazeez was employed with Superior Essex as a supervisor.

According to a representative of the family, Abdulazeez was abusing drugs and alcohol, preparing for bankruptcy, and facing an appearance in criminal court.[470]

The shootings began in mid-morning on July 16, 2015, at the Armed Forces Career Center in Chattanooga. Abdulazeez fired 30 to 45 shots into the office from inside a rented car, wounding a U.S. Marine. He then fled and led members of the Chattanooga Police Department on a pursuit. He drove to a U.S. Navy Reserve Center, where he rammed his car through a security gate. Driving to one of the center's buildings, he fired at it, then charged inside and continued firing. He fatally wounded sailor Randall Smith. He then left the building and entered a fenced motor pool area, where he shot several Marines.

Abdulazeez re-entered the building, firing upon responding police officers, and was fatally shot by them.[471]

Officials doing an Internet search on electronic devices owned by Abdulazeez indicated that he had done online research for militant Islamist "guidance" on committing violence that he may have believed would wipe away in the afterlife the sins he committed on earth.[472]

COVER

Gunnery Sgt. Camden Meyer, a Marine stationed in the recruiting center, shielded his daughter from gunfire. "I hit the floor," he said, "and immediately began to flatten my daughter's body as flat as it could go and shielding it with my body from the fire."[473]

EXIT

The same Marine who saved his daughter also protected a fellow colleague by ordering him not to run, and potentially protecting him from deadly gunfire. "I yelled at [Sgt. Winfield] Thompson to stay down until the break in fire. ...I know the shooter would have to switch weapons, change clips or reload."[474]

EXIT

Lance Cpl. Christopher Gilliam, the most junior Marine in the office, was first to spot the shooter and yelled to the others to run. "Run!" Gilliam yelled as the first rounds were fired into the office. He jumped over a cubicle and toward the back door. Once Gilliam exited, he headed down a hill and into a warehouse, where he called the police.

ASSESS

About 10 seconds later, Meyer heard Abdulazeez pause. He yelled to [Sgt.] Thompson that they needed to run. Meyer scooped up his daughter, and the three made it out the back door unharmed.[475]

Case #69 – Umpqua Community College	
Synopsis	26-year-old Chris Harper-Mercer opened fire inside a classroom at Umpqua Community College, killing nine people and injuring seven before dying in a shootout with police.
Type of Establishment	College Campus
Environment	Indoors
Motive	Unknown
Number killed	9
Number killed and injured	16
Date of murders	October 1, 2015
Weapon	Two handguns
Location	Roseburg, Oregon
Shooter status	Killed by police

Overview

Chris Harper-Mercer grew up in California and had attended a school for teenagers with learning disabilities or emotional problems. He lived with his mother during the separation and divorce of his parents, moving with her to Oregon for her job. He had joined the U.S. Army in 2008 but was discharged after only five weeks for failure to meet "minimum administrative standards" of basic training. He attended El Camino College from 2010 to 2012.[476]

Harper-Mercer lived with his mother in an apartment in which there were numerous legally purchased weapons. His mother had written in an online forum that both she and her son had Asperger syndrome, an autism spectrum disorder. The two were very close, and often spent time together at shooting ranges,[477] but Harper-Mercer was apparently extremely isolated otherwise and appeared to be unable to form deep connections with others.[478]

In the fall of 2015, Harper-Mercer was a student in a writing class at Umpqua Community College in Roseburg, Oregon. On October 1, he entered a classroom and fired a warning shot, telling the professor teaching the class, "I've been waiting to do this for years," then shooting him point blank. According to survivors, Mercer asked his hostages if they were Christians. "If they said yes, then they were shot in the head. If they said no or didn't answer, they were shot in the legs," a witness said.[479]

Harper-Mercer's writings discovered after the shooting include ramblings about his hostility toward black people, and general feelings of anger about being isolated and unable to form relationships.[480]

The killer had been placed on academic probation at school, and a September 1 letter warned him that he could be suspended if he did not raise his grades. He also owed tuition to the school.[481]

EXIT

Chris Mintz, an Army veteran who was shot five times during the rampage, said he held the door open as classmates ran toward the library, where he eventually followed and warned people there by running through the aisles shouting. He then ran back towards the campus' Snyder Hall, screaming at oblivious students to "get out of there, to leave."[482]

CONCEALMENT

Huddled together in a locked classroom, the students and teacher heard footsteps outside and a man's voice calling, "Come on out, come on out." They remained quiet and didn't open the door.[483]

Case #70 – Inland Regional Center

Synopsis	Syed Rizwan Farook, 28, and Tashfeen Malik, 27, opened fire at a San Bernardino County Department of Public Health training event and Christmas party.
Type of Establishment	County Building
Environment	Indoors
Motive	Terrorism
Number killed	14
Number killed and injured	35
Date of murders	December 2, 2015
Weapon	AR-15, 9mm handgun
Location	San Bernardino, California
Shooter status	Killed by police

Overview

Syed Rizwan Farook was a U.S.-born restaurant inspector for the San Bernardino County Health Department. His wife, Tashfeen Malik, was born in Pakistan but was a lawful permanent resident of the U.S. On the morning of December 2, 2015, they dropped off their 6-month-old daughter with relatives, then went to a social services center where the Health Department's holiday party was being held. Dressed for battle, Farook and Malik opened fire on those inside, killing 14 and seriously wounding more than a dozen others. Hours later, they died in a shootout with police.[484]

The pair was armed with two assault rifles and two handguns when they began their attack, and fired between 65 and 75 times. Inside the rental car in which the couple fled, police found more than 1600 rounds of ammunition. Another 4500 rounds were later found at their house.[485]

CONCEALMENT

Patrick Bacardi was in the restroom pulling a paper towel from a dispenser when he heard a blast and a puff of plaster dust flew from the wall as shards of the dispenser hit his face. He saw a hole in the wall. "Get down! Get down!" he yelled to the other men in the room. Bullets ripped into the towel dispenser as Bacardi dove for cover onto the floor. He and another man pushed the door closed with their legs and waited for police to arrive.

Denise Peraza and coworker Shannon Johnson huddled under a table, using a fallen chair as a shield. Johnson died, but Peraza, shot once in the lower back, survived.

Workers Corwin Porter and Trudy Raymundo noted that there were three exits in the conference room, but nobody tried to escape. "To stand up and go for the doors, you're in the line of sight of the gunman." They hid under tables and tried to stay as quiet as possible.[486]

CONCEALMENT/OTHER

Played dead

When the shooters entered the conference room, Amanda Gaspard dropped to the floor and hid under a table. Then she closed her eyes and lay motionless. She was shot in the lower arm, upper thigh and knee.[487]

COVER

"Olivia Navarro said her daughter, Jamile Navarro, a case manager at the social service center, called her and whispered that she was hiding in a locked room. 'I said, 'All right, I'll be there, turn off the lights, don't make a sound,' Navarro said. 'And that was it.' Her daughter survived."[488]

Case #71– Kalamazoo Community

Synopsis	45-year-old Jason Brian Dalton went on a series of apparently random shootings in an apartment complex, a car dealership, and outside a restaurant, leaving 6 people dead and two others critically injured.
Type of Establishment	Parking lots
Environment	Outdoors
Motive	Unknown
Number killed	6
Number killed and injured	8
Date of murders	February 20, 2016
Weapon	9mm Walther P99 semi-automatic with an extended magazine, and a 9mm Glock19 semi-automatic handgun
Location	Kalamazoo, Michigan
Shooter status	Charged with six counts of murder. As of February 2018, the case remains on hold pending an appeal to the Michigan Supreme Court.[489]

Overview

Jason Brian Dalton graduated with an associate degree in law enforcement from Kalamazoo Valley Community College in Michigan. He tried to seek a job as a police officer in Michigan and nearby states without success. He found jobs as an auto mechanic and then as an insurance adjuster. He had been counseled about his professionalism toward customers and had been witnessed yelling at customers over the phone.[490]

Dalton began working as a driver for Uber in early 2016, passing company background checks. On February 20, he confronted a woman in an apartment parking lot, asking if she was a person by another name. When she answered that she was not, he fired repeatedly at her, but she survived. Ten shell casings were recovered at the scene.

Some four hours later, Dalton arrived at a car dealership in Kalamazoo, where he shot and killed two people. A witness said that the shooter approached the victims and talked with them and then opened fire. About 15 minutes later, four people inside two vehicles at a nearby Cracker Barrel restaurant were killed, and one person wounded.

Neighbors said that Dalton had been acting paranoid before the shootings. In the hours before the shootings, he went to a gun store and purchased a black jacket with a chest pocket designed to conceal a handgun.[491]

A woman whose fiancé had gotten a ride from Dalton before the first shooting said that the driver had been acting irrationally and driving erratically, sideswiping a car and running through traffic signals at high speeds.[492]

Police identified Dalton as the suspect and arrested him without incident. He confessed to the shootings and told police that the Uber app had forced him to go on the killing spree. He said that when he opened the app, he "recognized the Uber symbol as being that of the Eastern star" and that a "devil head" would pop up on his screen. He said that was "when all the problems started."[493]

Another 15 firearms were recovered from Dalton's home.

CONCEALMENT

Alexis Cornish, 17, witnessed the shooting at the Ford KIA Dealership that killed her boyfriend and his father. She described how her boyfriend and his father fell down after they were shot, and she hid behind a car seat. She then grabbed her boyfriend's phone from his pocket and dialed 911 as both her boyfriend and his father lay still.[494]

OTHER

Played Dead

Tiana Carruthers was shot but survived, and later recounted how she began to run and then played dead.[495]

CASE #72 – PULSE NIGHTCLUB	
Synopsis	U.S. citizen Omar Mateen, age 29, opened fire in a crowded gay nightclub in the early morning hours of June 12, 2016, killing 49 and wounding 53.
Historical Note	The Pulse nightclub shooting is the 2nd deadliest mass shooting by a single shooter in U.S. history, and the deadliest terrorist attack since 9/11/2001.
Type of Establishment	Nightclub
Environment	Indoors
Motive	Terrorism
Number killed	49
Number killed and injured	102
Date of murders	June 12, 2016
Weapon	Sig Sauer semi-automatic rifle; 9mm Glock 17 semi-automatic pistol
Location	Orlando, Florida
Shooter status	Killed by police after a three-hour standoff/hostage situation

Overview

Omar Mateen was born in New York. His parents were Afghan and he was raised as a Muslim. In 2006 and 2007 he trained to be a prison guard for the Florida Department of Corrections. He had failed in his attempt to be a Florida state trooper in 2011 and to be admitted to a police academy in 2015. He had an active statewide firearms license and an active security officer license, had passed a psychological test, and had no criminal record.[496]

Mateen married in 2009 but his wife left him after a few months; their divorce was final two years later. After the nightclub shootings, she described him a “mentally unstable and mentally ill,” said that he had been verbally and physically abusive during their relationship. She said that he had never expressed sympathy for terrorist organizations or radical Islamists, but did make anti-gay comments when he was angry.[497] At the time of the shootings, Mateen was married to his second wife and had a young son.

A former co-worker of Mateen's said that he had talked about killing people, used slurs, and seemed to have a lot of hatred for blacks, women, Jews, Hispanics, and gays and lesbians.

On June 12, 2016, Mateen drove to Orlando to the Pulse nightclub, a popular gay hangout. That night was Latin Night and most of the more than 300 in attendance were Hispanic. Mateen approached the building carrying a SIG Sauer semi-automatic rifle and a 9mm Glock 17 semi-automatic pistol. A uniformed security guard engaged him; Mateen passed by him into the building.

Mateen began firing indiscriminately. People began fleeing frantically, but many couldn't escape. About 20 minutes into the attack, Mateen called 911 and pledged his allegiance to the Islamic State. He directed the hostage negotiator to tell the U.S. to stop bombing ISIL.

Mateen held the remaining clubgoers hostage. One survivor reported that after Mateen called 911, he asked if there were any black people in the bathroom. He said, "…I don't have any problem with black people. You guys have suffered enough."[498]

After about three hours, a SWAT team broke through the back wall of the club in an armored vehicle, and engaged in a shootout with Mateen, who was killed at just before 6:00 a.m.[499] Just before the breach, Mateen opened fire on people hiding inside a women's bathroom, killing at least two inside.

EXIT

Imran Yousuf was a recently-discharged Marine veteran working as a bouncer at Pulse. When he heard gunfire, he immediately recognized the sounds as being from a high caliber gun. He ran toward a locked door that people had huddled around, too terrified to move, even as he screamed "Open the door! Open the door!" He jumped over to open the latch and an estimated 70 people were thus able to escape.[500]

Christopher Hansen, a clubgoer who was inside when the shooting began, told the AP that he escaped through the back of the venue by crawling on his elbows and knees.[501]

Some people escaped through the emergency exit. Some people escaped through the patio. Ashley Summers was ordering drinks from the bar when she heard a popping sound; it went on for 15 seconds before her friend pulled her to the ground. Ms. Summers and her friends escaped by crawling out the patio exit nearby.

While the gunman was on the phone with police, more people fled. At least four people in a dressing room escaped from an exit on the north side. The police also helped eight people in another dressing room escape through an air conditioner vent.[502]

CONCEALMENT

Some people ran to hide in the bathrooms where the standoff ensued. "People were screaming, begging for their lives," said one patron. He took cover with a friend in a cramped bathroom stall, hiding on top of the toilet so their feet could not be seen from the outside.[503]

One young woman who was trapped in the bathroom with numerous other victims crawled under several dead bodies, concealing herself and staying out of sight from the shooter.[504]

ASSESS/EXIT

Multiple individuals who were concealing themselves behind a bar out of the shooter's line of vision noticed that he had moved away from the initial point of attack and took the opportunity to escape out a door to safety.

ASSESS/CONCEALMENT

Yvens Carrenards turned to run for safety when he noticed a ladder leading to an attic-like area. He and several others climbed into the area and barricaded the door. "It was sort of a storage room," he said. He called for help on his phone, and he and the others huddled together waiting for rescue.[505]

Case #73 – Dallas Protest Rally

Synopsis	Micah Xavier Johnson, age 25, ambushed and fired upon police officers who were providing security and crowd control for a peaceful rally and march protesting recent police killings in Louisiana and Minnesota.
Type of Establishment	Parade Route
Environment	Outdoors
Motive	Racial
Number killed	5
Number killed and injured	16
Date of murders	July 7, 2016
Weapon	Semi-automatic rifle, handgun
Location	Dallas, Texas
Shooter status	Killed by police

Overview

Mississippi-born Micah Xavier Johnson was raised in Mesquite, Texas, a suburb of Dallas. He struggled academically and was ranked 430th out of the 453 students in his 2009 graduating class. He had enrolled in classes at a community college but never completed any of them.

After graduation, Johnson enlisted in the U.S. Army Reserve and served from March 2009 to April 2015. He was deployed to Afghanistan between November 2013 and July 2014. He was sent home from Afghanistan in 2014 after being accused of sexual harassment by a female soldier, but he was never convicted of any criminal offense and was honorably discharged in 2015.[506]

A friend and former coworker described Johnson as "always distrustful of the police."[507] Another described him a very affected by recent police shootings of black men. It was learned that he had demonstrated online interest in Black Nationalist groups, and a few days before the attack he had posted an angry post against white people.

The Next Generation Action Network had organized a peaceful protest scheduled for July 7 in downtown Dallas on behalf of the Black Lives Matter movement, in recognition of recent police killings of black men in Louisiana and Minnesota. Dallas police officers were on scene observing and protecting the event and the surrounding area. The event was peaceful, and a number of officers engaged in friendly conversation with protestors.

Just before 9:00 p.m., as the protest was ending, Micah Johnson pulled his SUV onto Lamar Street at the east entrance to El Centro Community College. There, the school's Police Chief Joseph Hannigan said, he started a conversation with three Dallas police officers. "He got out and we believe, engaged three Dallas police officers in a short conversation, then pulled his rifle and shot them," Hannigan said.[508]

Taking cover at street level, Johnson began shooting at groups of police and protesters who were gathered on Main Street. After being wounded by return fire, he tried to enter the Lamar Street entrance of El Centro by shooting out its glass door but was unable to gain access. He wounded two campus police officers who were inside the building. He then went to Elm Street, shot out another door and entered the college.

Hearing the sound of glass shattering, Cpl. Bryan Shaw entered the building and discovered a trail of blood leading to a stairwell. Shaw and another officer entered the stairwell and were met with gunfire from above. The officers retreated.

Meanwhile, Johnson made his way through the building, shooting out multiple windows and firing at police officers down on Elm Street. He hit one officer standing in front of a convenience store, killing him. Officers began entering the college buildings, sealing off escape routes and evacuating students and teachers.

Johnson was ultimately discovered to be on the second floor behind a corner in an area filled with offices and the school's computer servers. SWAT was on scene and exchanged gunfire with Johnson.

Dallas police attempted to negotiate with Johnson, who said he would speak to black officers only. He said that he was acting alone and not as a member of any group. After hours of standoff, it became clear that further negotiations were pointless, and the use of a bomb disposal remote control vehicle armed with C-4 explosive was authorized. As the robot approached him, Johnson fired at it repeatedly, but it exploded and killed him in the early morning hours of July 8.

EXIT

As the chaos erupted, half of the crowd ran off to the left, the other half ran to the right. "You see police officers rushing people off the street, people who froze, telling people to get to the buildings to seek cover," said Sharay Santora.[509]

COVER

When the gunfire rang out, Shetamia Taylor shielded her boys, throwing herself in front of them so they could run to safety. At least one bullet hit Taylor's right calf as she covered one of her sons, 15, on the ground.

Lynn Mays reported to The Dallas Morning News, "All of a sudden we started hearing gunshots, just out of nowhere. At first we couldn't identify it because we wasn't expecting it. Then we started hearing more rapid fire." He said, "One police officer that was standing there pushed me out [of] the way because [the shooting] was coming our direction." Cuts, still bloody, on Mays's legs showed where he fell when he was pushed out of harm's way. "When the officer pushed me out [of] the way, next thing you know, we heard, 'Officer down,'" Mays told the newspaper.[510]

Several people said officers helped save them, including one man who said an officer pushed him out of the way as shooting began. Bystanders captured footage of cops dragging fallen comrades out of the line of fire.[511]

CASE #74– CASCADE SHOPPING MALL	
Synopsis	Arcan Cetin, age 20, opened fire inside the Cascade Mall, killing five. He was taken into custody.
Type of Establishment	Shopping mall
Environment	Indoors
Motive	Unknown
Number killed	5
Number killed and injured	5
Date of murders	September 23, 2016
Weapon	.22 caliber Ruger rifle
Location	Burlington, Washington
Shooter status	Charged with murder and held for mental competency evaluation. Committed suicide in jail on April 16, 2017.[512]

Overview

Turkish-born Arcan Cetin immigrated to the U.S. with his parents when he was six. He grew up in and still lived in Oak Harbor, Washington. He had a criminal record that included three domestic-violence assault charges relating to his stepfather and had been told by a judge that he was not to possess a firearm. He attempted suicide in November of 2015 and was hospitalized for two weeks.[513]

A neighbor who lived in a nearby apartment said she was so frightened by Cetin that she complained to apartment management and kept a stun gun handy. "He was really creepy, rude and obnoxious," and said that she tried to avoid him.[514]

On September 23, 2016, Cetin carried a Ruger rifle into a Macy's store in the Cascade Mall in Burlington, Washington and opened fire, killing four and wounding a man who died the next day. Cetin placed the rifle on top of a counter and fled the store. He was caught the next day walking along a road in Oak Harbor, and charged with five counts of first-degree murder. He confessed to the crimes but gave no explanation for his actions.[515]

CONCEALMENT

"The cashier…said he's got a gun, run! So I ran back into the dressing room with my daughter," said Melissa Rodriguez. They hid in the dressing room just seconds after the gunman killed his first victim.[516]

CASE #75 – FORT LAUDERDALE AIRPORT	
Synopsis	Esteban Santiago, 26, opened fire in an airport terminal, killing 5 and wounding 6.
Type of Establishment	Airport
Environment	Indoors
Motive	Unknown
Number killed	5
Number killed and injured	11
Date of murders	January 6, 2017
Weapon	Walther PPS 9mm semi-automatic pistol
Location	Fort Lauderdale, Florida
Shooter status	Awaiting trial

Overview

Esteban Santiago served as a combat engineer in the National Guard in Puerto Rico and Alaska but was discharged from service for unsatisfactory performance. He had been reported for several infractions. During his time with the Guard, he was deployed to Iraq from April 2010 to February 2011.[517]

During 2016 Santiago was repeatedly reported to Anchorage police for disturbances, including two reports of domestic violence and strangulation. In November of that year, he went to an FBI office in Anchorage to report that "his mind was being controlled by a U.S. intelligence agency" and that he "believed he was being influenced by ISIS." He was transported for medical evaluation.[518] The FBI closed their investigation on Santiago, having found no ties to terrorism.

On January 6, 2017, Santiago flew Delta from Anchorage to Fort Lauderdale. He had checked a semi-automatic handgun with TSA per protocol. Upon landing, he retrieved the gun from baggage claim, loaded the weapon in the restroom, and then opened fire in Terminal 2 of the Fort Lauderdale airport. According to a witness, he "went up and down the carousels of the baggage claim, shooting through luggage to get at people that were hiding."[519]

When Santiago ran out of ammunition, he lay down on the floor and he was taken into custody by a sheriff's deputy. Five people were dead, six wounded, and more than 30 people were injured in the panic during the shooting.

EXIT

Passenger David Fogarty was heading out on vacation when people around him suddenly began running toward the gates. "Everybody was dropping gear, panicking, jumping over tables," Fogarty said.[520]

CONCEALMENT

Traveler Tara Webber was waiting in Terminal 3 for her flight home to Pennsylvania. She and her father dived under a set of plastic chairs. Ms. Webber said she almost landed on a little girl, who was crying, and tried to comfort her.[521]

CASE #76 – AWNING FACTORY

Synopsis	John R. Neumann, Jr., 45, shot five people at his former workplace and then turned the gun on himself.
Type of Establishment	Factory
Environment	Indoor
Motive	Unknown/Revenge
Number killed	5
Number killed and injured	5
Date of murders	June 5, 2017
Weapon	Semi-automatic pistol
Location	Orlando, Florida
Shooter status	Committed suicide

Overview

John Robert Neumann was a 45-year-old Army veteran who lived alone. He worked for Fiamma, Inc., which manufactures awnings for camper vans, motor coaches and sport utility vehicles. In 2014 Neumann was accused of battering a co-worker and was investigated by authorities, but no charges were filed. He had a record of minor crimes, most involving traffic violations, but no violent offenses.[522]

Neumann was fired from his job in April of 2017. A neighbor of his said that "He seemed to be angry. He seemed like he complained a lot." At about 8:00 a.m. on June 5, Neumann entered the cavernous factory through a rear door and began methodically firing, killing four and wounding one before turning the pistol on himself. The wounded man later died at the hospital. [523]

When the shooting began, an employee ran out and called 911 from a business across the street. Law enforcement officers arrived on scene within minutes.

Sheriff Jerry Demings stated that "Most of the victims were shot in the head; some were shot multiple times."[524] The co-worker with whom Neumann had previously tangled was not among the victims.

EXIT

Gunman's choice

A woman ran out and called 911 from a business across the street, according to the store's owner. "All she kept saying was he was holding a gun and told her to get out."[525]

Case #77 – Harvest Music Festival	
Synopsis	Stephen Paddock, 64, rented a 32nd-floor hotel suite from which he fired upon those attending an outdoor concert several streets away.
Historical Note	This was the deadliest single-day mass shooting in U.S. history.
Type of Establishment	Concert area
Environment	Outdoors
Motive	Unknown
Number killed	58
Number killed and injured	480[vi]
Date of murders	October 1, 2017
Weapon	Automatic rifle
Location	Las Vegas, Nevada
Shooter status	Committed suicide

Overview

Stephen Paddock held various federal jobs in the 1970s and 80s, working for the U.S. Postal Service, the Internal Revenue Service, and the Defense Contract Audit Agency. He had made a small fortune in real estate and business deals in Nevada, Florida, California and Texas. When he purchased a home in Mesquite, Nevada, a retirement community about 80 miles from Las Vegas, he told the real estate agent that he gambled about $1 million a year. Some of his neighbors knew that he was a gambler, but knew little more about him, since he kept a very low profile.[526]

[vi] The preliminary report released by the Clark County Sheriff in January 2018 indicated that 422 people suffered injuries as a direct result of gunfire, and another 851 individuals suffered other injuries in the attack. See https://www.cnn.com/2018/01/19/us/las-vegas-shooting-investigation-update/index.html

In the last week of September 2017, Paddock checked into the Mandalay Bay Resort and Casino near the end of the Las Vegas Strip. He ultimately moved into a two-room suite on the 32nd floor corner which spread out over 1700 square feet and featured floor-to-ceiling windows.[527] The 10 suitcases he brought with him contained at least 23 weapons including multiple rifles, some with scopes. A hotel worker reported that a "Do Not Disturb" sign hung on the door for more than three days, so housekeepers did not enter the room.[528]

Paddock placed cameras as monitors, one in the peephole and two in the hallway (apparently to watch for police). At some point he barricaded the doors to his room and the stairwell.

September 29 was the first night of the Route 91 Harvest Festival, held at the Las Vegas Village and Festival Grounds northeast of the Mandalay Bay. The outdoor festival drew more than 20,000 concertgoers. Country star Jason Aldean was the closing act on October 1, and his set began at about 9:40 p.m.

At around 10:00 p.m., Mandalay Bay security guard Jesus Campos went to the 32nd floor to investigate a reported open door. Paddock apparently detected Campos via surveillance camera, and he fired through the door and wounded the unarmed guard.[529]

At 10:05 p.m., the first burst of gunfire sprayed over the crowd. Gunfire erupted repeatedly in rapid-fire bursts. Paddock continued firing for about ten minutes.

Thirteen minutes after the first shooting, police officers were on the way to confront the gunman. Eighteen minutes after the attack began, two Las Vegas Metro Police Department officers found wounded guard Campos, who told them which room the shooter was in. More officers soon arrived and began searching nearby rooms and evacuating guests. Police wanted to enter the shooter's room but were told to wait for SWAT. As police later explained, "The floor had been evacuated of any guests; the suspect was contained and isolated within a room."[530]

At 11:20 p.m., police broke into Paddock's room and found him dead of a self-inflicted gunshot wound. They recovered 23 guns from the suite, including handguns and high-powered rifles capable of piercing police armor. A later search of his home turned up another 19 fire-arms, explosives, and several rounds of ammunition. Paddock's car contained several pounds of ammonium nitrate, an ingredient used in explosives.[531]

Most of the weapons were legally purchased since October 2016 in gun shops in Nevada, Arizona, Utah and Texas.[532] At the time of this writing, law enforcement authorities had still not discovered a motive for Paddock's rampage.

EXIT

Jamey Eller said she and her friends hit the ground with the first fusillade, and then "the second round came and we started to belly crawl." Then they got up and ran.[533]

Some survivors tried to climb the chain-link fence topped with barbed wire around the nearby McCarran Airport, until firefighters ripped the fence up from the ground, allowing them to crawl under it.[534]

Fellow concertgoers helped Elle Gargano get over the fence and out of the festival grounds, and a passerby drove her to the hospital.[535]

EXIT
Helped others

Off-duty Clark County firefighter Jesse Gomez was enjoying the concert with his wife and other relatives when the shooting started. They began running to the east side of the venue, away from the gunfire. They came across a woman who was bleeding from her head and face. "We just picked her up and we carried her to the other side, me and a couple of strangers," Jessie said. He returned to the concert venue, and physically carried out six to ten people on his own.[536]

EXIT
Locked down

Krystal Legette was at the Sundance Helicopters office at the airport, waiting for a sightseeing flight, when three women burst into the building, screaming, "They're shooting, they're shooting!" Another woman came in, bleeding from a bullet wound in her arm. Then more people ran into the office, until finally about 100 had taken shelter there. A worker turned out the lights, locked the doors and told everyone to go inside closets and other areas away from windows.[537]

COVER

As Debbie Gomez and family members fled and ran to their car, they realized that about 10 people were using it as a shield.[538]

After Ella Gargano was shot in the head, her friend got her under the stage to protect her. Ella survived.[539]

CONCEALMENT

John Phippen was at the festival with his son Travis when the shooting started. When the son, a medic, stopped to help someone, Phippen stayed with him and was shielding a woman when he was shot dead.[540]

Jack Beaton was celebrating his 23rd anniversary with his wife Laurie when the gunfire started. He told her to get on the ground and draped his body over her to protect her. He was hit, and died, but Laurie survived.[541]

Case #78 – First Baptist Church	
Synopsis	Devin Patrick Kelley, age 26, began shooting at the First Baptist Church before entering the building to gun down the congregation during the morning service.
Historical Note	This was the deadliest mass shooting in Texas history, and the 5th deadliest mass shooting in U.S. history.
Type of Establishment	Church
Environment	Indoors
Motive	Unknown
Number killed	26
Number killed and injured	46
Date of murders	November 5, 2017
Weapon	Ruger assault-style rifle
Location	Sutherland Springs, Texas
Shooter status	Committed suicide

Overview

Devin Patrick Kelley served in the U.S. Air Force, but was court-martialed in 2012 for an assault on his first wife and his stepson. He received a bad conduct discharge and a reduction in rank, and was held in confinement for 12 months.[542] His wife, from whom he was divorced in 2012, described him as a "menacing and abusive man" who constantly threatened her and her family with death.[543]

In 2012, Kelley escaped from a mental health facility after being caught sneaking guns onto an Air Force base "attempting to carry out death threats" against military superiors. His history included charges of animal cruelty, mental health concerns, investigations for domestic assault, and threats against his family members.[544]

In early 2014, El Paso County, Colorado police investigated a domestic violence complaint involving Kelley and his then-girlfriend, but no charges were filed. He and the girlfriend married that year.

By 2017 Kelley and his wife were in Texas. He worked briefly as an unarmed security guard at a water park, a job that required him to pass a criminal background check, but was terminated just shy of six weeks on the job.[545]

Kelley's domestic violence conviction should have been reported to the FBI, but the Air Force acknowledged that it failed to relay that information. Thus between 2014 and 2017, Kelley was able to purchase a Ruger AR-556 rifle and at least two other firearms; on the background check paperwork, he checked the box to indicate that he had no disqualifying criminal history, and his name did not appear in NICS, the federal database against which firearms purchases are checked.

In his second marriage, Kelley apparently had problems with his in-laws, and had sent his mother-in-law threatening texts. Kelley's wife and her parents attended the small First Baptist Church in Sutherland Springs, about 35 miles from Kelley's home in New Braunfels.

On the morning of November 5, Kelley dressed in tactical gear and armed himself with the Ruger rifle, then drove to the First Baptist Church. He began shooting from outside as he approached the church, and then entered the building where he continued shooting those attending the 11:00 a.m. service.

One of the wounded later said that Kelley fired at those who tried to leave, and at those cowering or wounded on the floor. He reloaded several times and appeared to have emptied 15 magazines.[546] When the shooting stopped, 26 people (including the unborn child of one woman) were dead and more than 20 were wounded. The victims ranged in age from 18 months to 77 years.

As the gunman left the church, town resident Stephen Willeford grabbed his own rifle and confronted him and fired at him. Kelley dropped his gun and fled in his vehicle, and Willeford and another man chased Kelley down the road, where he eventually crashed his car. Authorities found him dead, apparently from a self-inflicted gunshot wound.

Kelley's in-laws had not attended church that day.

CONCEALMENT

Zach Poston, 18, was shot while lying on the ground. He saw a young girl hiding under a pew about to run out, but he kicked her back underneath.[547]

OTHER

Played dead

Survivor Rosanne Solis described her terror as Kelley fired at people even after they had already been shot. "I knew if I said something he was gonna kill me." She prayed for help and played dead so as not to attract his attention. "...I made sure that I hid myself good under [a] bench," adding that a boy and a woman hid with her. Solis was hit by a bullet but survived.[548]

Case #79 – Marjory Douglas High School	
Synopsis	Nikolas Cruz, 19, entered the campus of Marjory Stoneman Douglas High School and conducted one of the deadliest school shootings in U.S. history.
Historical Note	This was the 3rd deadliest school shooting in U.S. history.
Type of Establishment	School
Environment	Indoors
Motive	Unknown
Number killed	17
Number killed and injured	33
Date of murders	February 14, 2018
Weapon	AR-15 semi-automatic rifle
Location	Parkland, Florida
Shooter status	Committed suicide with bomb

Overview

Nikolas Cruz witnessed his adoptive father's death when he was 6. As a child he was diagnosed with depression, attention deficit hyperactivity disorder, emotional behavioral disability, and autism. His adoptive mother said that had obsessive-compulsive disorder and anger issues. In eighth grade Cruz was assigned to a school for students with emotional problems. He had trouble making friends and was bullied.

Although Cruz was very close to his mother Lynda, there were times that he got physical with her and his brother. Palm Beach County Sheriff's deputies responded to 23 calls to the home over a 10-year period.[549]

By 16, Nikolas was fascinated with wars, death and killing. He was not happy at the new school and begged to be allowed to attend Marjory Stoneman Douglas High School, one of the best in the district. The school district allowed his enrollment at Douglas. During his first month there, he posted on Instagram that he planned to shoot up the school.

Cruz completed 10th grade at Douglas, but in his junior year he had multiple difficulties. He was suspended for fighting. He was reported to the state for cutting his arms. He said he wanted to buy a gun. He had a Nazi symbol and a racist comment on his book bag.

In November of 2016, Lynda Cruz died of pneumonia. With no parents, Nikolas and his brother were taken in by former neighbor Rocxanne Deschamps, but she couldn't let Nikolas remain. She said that he was violent, that he had eight guns kept at a friend's house, and a bulletproof vest. Another family in Parkland, the Sneads, took him in, insisting that he keep his weapons locked up.[550]

In January 2017, Cruz assaulted someone at Douglas and was suspended and transferred to an alternative school. On January 5 a caller told the FBI about one of Cruz's Instagram posts that said, "I want to kill people," and told them that he had once pulled a rifle on his mother.

On February 14, Cruz told the Sneads that he'd be skipping school, not wanting to go to school on Valentine's Day. At 2:06 p.m., Cruz caught an Uber to Douglas High, arriving as school was letting out. He entered Building 12 carrying an AR-15 rifle in a black case. He encountered a freshman in a second-floor hallway and told him, "You'd better get out of here. Things are gonna start getting messy."[551] The student fled.

When the shooting started at just after 2:20 p.m., the school went into a lockdown procedure called Code Red, where hallway fire doors are locked and students and teachers stay in their classrooms. But fire alarms went off and overrode the Code Red. Assistant football coach Aaron Feis went running down a hallway and pushed students to safety. He was shot and killed.

Cruz fired into multiple classrooms, killing and wounding students and their teachers. After less than 10 minutes, he exited Building 12 and ran with other students who were fleeing. He then went to a Walmart and bought a drink at the Subway restaurant inside. He left there at about 3:00 p.m. and went to a McDonald's, where he sat for a while, and left on foot. At 3:41 p.m., he was spotted on the street and detained by a Coconut Creek police officer. After being identified by witnesses, he was arrested.[552]

In the attack lasting less than 10 minutes, 17 were dead and 16 were wounded.

EXIT

Student Peter Wang held a door open to let other students out of the building before him. He was shot and killed.[553]

CONCEALMENT

Algebra teacher Shanthi Viswanathan placed paper over the classroom window so that no one could see in and told students to get on the floor in the corner.

Hearing the shots, geography teacher Scott Beigel unlocked a door to a classroom to let students hide inside. Beigel was shot and killed.[554]

OTHER

Barricaded door

As the gunman came upon the classroom and began shooting, 15-year-old Anthony Borges was trapped in a classroom with 20 others. Anthony barricaded the door with his body, preventing Cruz from entering. Everyone in the room survived, but Anthony was shot five times.[555]

Precursor to the ESCAPE Model: unique observations of actions taken by survivors of mass shootings

In reviewing each of the case studies and analyzing them through the prism of three decades in law enforcement, I found several commonalities evident with regard to the instinctive actions taken and conscious tactics implemented by victims of mass shooting attacks. Some instinctual actions were the correct path to safety, while others may have increased the level of victimization.

This section examines some of the common victim responses—whether instinctive or conscious—and how those actions or tactics helped or hurt those involved. For example: for years, academicians have told us that one of our most basic instincts when faced with imminent danger is "fight or flight." These instinctual actions are also two-thirds of the Department of Homeland Security Active Shooter response model. However, research clearly indicates that fighting—especially by an untrained, unarmed individual—rarely results in a safe and successful conclusion to the event. In fact, this type of response almost always leads to the injury or death of the individual attempting to stop the shooter's rampage. More detailed information on fighting an armed offender as a response during a mass shooting is presented in the *Engage* portion of the ESCAPE Model later in this text.

On the other hand, certain tactics such as playing dead have worked on occasion for multiple individuals, some of whom stated that they saw the tactic on television, and others who just thought it seemed like a good idea at the time. Other tactics which seem just as reasonable, such as pleading for one's life, have failed most of the time.

Armed with these vital observations, citizens will be able to learn from past incidents, and understand both successful and unsuccessful tactics which have been utilized by victims in such events.

Successful Tactics

An examination of successful tactics taken by individuals who have survived a mass shooting reveals that:

- Locked or barricaded doors can slow or stop offenders; and
- Playing dead (whether actually wounded or not) can save your life.

Both of these tactics have been successfully employed by victims during mass shootings or active shooter incidents.

1. *Locked/barricaded doors can slow or stop offenders.*

On multiple occasions, especially in schools and workplaces, locking or barricading doors has proven to be a highly successful tactic. If you have an opportunity to lock the door with the offender on the outside, **do so immediately**. If you do not feel that the lock will stop the shooter and you can safely move to barricade the door with chairs, tables, couches or other furniture, then do so.

You may be able to topple file cabinets (even if heavy) or other large items in order to impede the shooter's path towards you. Often these obstructions will also serve as either cover or concealment and may frustrate the shooter in his attempt to enter so that he moves on to easier targets.

Remember, mass shootings are usually not prolonged events. They often take less than 12 minutes, so the offender usually does not have (or take) the time to shoot open a door and knock down a barricade in order to make entry. Reports from survivors often recount how the shooter tried the lock or pushed on the door, but when unable to gain entry simply moved on, sparing the occupants inside. This is one of the main reasons school districts throughout the country practice lockdown procedures, and why corporations should implement these same successful tactics.[vii]

Case #37. **An attempt to break into an English classroom was thwarted by a quick-thinking teacher who had taken the precaution to lock the door. This execution of one of the safety procedures established by the school saved many lives.**

Case #54. **The owner of a salon two doors away from the location of the shootings said she and her customers and employees heard gunshots, and her receptionist saw a man through a window as he was shot in a parking lot. "There was like a pop, pop and my receptionist screamed, 'he just shot that man' and we all ran into the bathroom and locked the door," Kimberly Criswell said.**

Case #60. **First grade teacher Kaitlin Roig hid 14 students in a bathroom and barricaded the door, telling them to be completely quiet to remain safe.**

2. *Playing dead has worked on a number of occasions.*

From the case analyses, I was surprised to discover that playing dead provided an extremely high survival chance during a shooting incident, whether the victims were previously injured or not. Upon closer analysis of these events I realized that there is more than reasonable logic behind such a finding: during a mass shooting incident, especially when the shooter has a large number of targets (people) from which to choose, playing dead would draw the least attention from the shooter.

Often, shooters appear to be on a "mission" to kill as many people as possible. If they believe they have already fatally wounded their targets, they may simply keep moving on to other victims instead of ensuring that those already shot are dead. Mass shootings are usually very fast-moving events, and in some cases such as in the Emanuel AME church shooting in Charleston, South Carolina (which lasted only

---

[vii] **NOTE**: Many of the case references which follow appeared in the previous Case Studies and are referenced in the End Notes. Those anecdotes or reports which did not appear in previous chapters will show End Note references here.

about 90 seconds), the assailant even asked some of the victims if he had already shot them, not knowing who he had attacked in the group of worshippers.

Although some shooters are slow and methodical in their attacks, often these killers move quickly through a location and do not take the time to check on each victim. The possible exception to this might be if the shooter had a specific target or primary victim(s) in mind, such as a student who bullied them or a boss who fired them, and they wanted to ensure that their attack had been successfully concluded.

It is important to note that there appears to be no unified explanation as to why certain people decided to play dead. Some did it as a result of extreme fear, some did it because of they were badly injured or immobilized, and some did it as a conscious strategy to stay alive.

Case #4. Joshua Coleman, 11, was riding his bike to McDonald's and heard the [shooter] yell. He turned and he was hit. Lying on the pavement, his right side riddled with shotgun pellets, and the gunman still shooting, Joshua played dead. How did he know to do so? "I don't know," he says. "I got lucky. The fact he kept shooting at us. . . You hear about an accident and sometimes you think, 'What would you do if you were there?' and I always thought I would play dead."

Case#16. The first gunshot victim, Mary Anne Phillips, testified that she had played dead after being wounded. She said she kept her eyes closed so that [the shooter] would not come back and shoot her again.

Case #21. Lelan Brookins survived the massacre by playing dead.

Case #27. Isaiah Shoels, Matthew Kechter and Craig Scott were hiding underneath a table. Harris knelt down and shot Shoels once in the chest at close range, killing him. Klebold also knelt down and opened fire, hitting and killing Matthew Kechter. Craig Scott lay next to his friends and played dead and was uninjured.

Mark Taylor was shot in the chest, arms and leg and fell to the ground, where he played dead and survived.

Case #37. Lance Crowe, 15, survived by playing dead, lying among those killed.

Case #49. Receptionist Shirley DeLucia was one of the first to be shot, being hit in the stomach. She then pretended to be dead and, when the gunman moved on, hid under a desk and called 911.

Case #57. Moviegoer Corbin Dates crawled on the floor to try to get out. He urged others to pretend that they were dead.

Chandler Brannon realized that the noises he was hearing were gunshots. "I told my girlfriend to just play dead," he said.

Case #60. First grade substitute teacher Lauren Rousseau and all but one of the children in her classroom were shot dead. The sole survivor, a six-year-old girl, played dead and remained still until the building was quiet and she thought it was safe to leave. She was the first child to escape the building.

Most Common Concerns

An examination of actions taken by those involved in mass shootings revealed two primary areas of concern:

1. Pleading for your life rarely works, and
2. Not realizing what was occurring slowed the responses by individuals.

Becoming aware of these facts will add to your personal database of knowledge and, ideally, better prepare you if you are ever faced with a mass shooting incident.

Pleading for your life rarely works.

There have been several cases where individuals caught in the killer's line of sight with nowhere to run or hide have pleaded for their lives or the lives of others. More often than not, those pleas fell on deaf ears—or, more correctly, on non-empathetic ears.

For years, researchers studying the psychology of various types of killers have listed *lack of empathy for others* as a common characteristic. Because of this, it should not come as a surprise that pleading for one's life is often a futile tactic. Most of these killers act as if they are on a mission, with a goal of securing as high a body count as possible. Seldom over the past 30 years has a mass murderer decided to spare someone's life in an out- of-character act of compassion.

Additionally, individuals who unnecessarily exposed themselves to the assailant to beg for mercy for themselves or others often found themselves targeted, with the ultimate result that they became a victim. If one understands an offender's lack of empathy for his victims, then any other decision, such as remaining concealed or playing dead, may provide a better opportunity for survival.

Case #15. **Restaurant proprietor Pete Parrous approached [the gunman] and asked him not to hurt anyone. Parrous was shot in the face and died instantly. As he fell, his wife stood up screaming and she was shot too. She fell beside her daughter, who began screaming and who was shot in the thigh.**

Wesley Cover had been tending to a patron who had been hit by a pellet from the shooting. He asked the gunman not to hurt the woman he was helping because she was pregnant. Mr. Cover was then shot in the head and died. The woman was also shot, but not fatally.

Case #17. **Customer Colleen O'Connor saw [the gunman] coming and knelt in front of him to beg for her life. As she raised her arms, he held a gun just 18 inches from her head. "Don't shoot," she cried. "I won't tell." "I have to," the shooter said as he pulled the trigger.**

Case #24. **Lottery president Otho Brown ran from the building with Beck in pursuit. Brown stumbled in the parking lot, apparently after losing a shoe. He fell to the ground, raised his hands, and begged "Don't kill me, don't kill me," to which Beck answered, "Aw, shut up," and shot him.**

Case #54. **Randy Fannin...was the first person to be shot, and he died. He reportedly said to the gunman, "Please don't do this. There's another way. Let's go outside and talk." Dekraii [the gunman] said "Shut up" and continued firing.**

Not realizing what was occurring slowed responses by individuals.

In conducting research for this book, reading through each of the cases in rapid succession without trying to consciously look for commonalities or attempting to over-process the information, I found that several themes became quite evident. One of the most common occurrences was that at the beginning of a shooting, it took some people a few moments to realize a shooting had occurred. I contend that the reason for the delayed response is that *most people have never heard gunfire or been involved in any type of violent incident.*

On numerous occasions, victims mistook gunfire or even explosions as firecrackers, pranks or part of some type of play, holiday celebration or promotional stunt, causing their initial response to be delayed by valuable seconds or even minutes.

In a mass shooting situation, every second counts, and even the slightest delay in response can have dire consequences. For this reason, after the Columbine High School massacre law enforcement agencies throughout the county changed their policies and procedures in an effort to speed up response to active shooter events. Response time is critical during these situations, and new active shooter protocols are centered on dynamic entry to reduce response time and quickly conclude the incident.

Individuals must be able to quickly recognize the situation and respond. If you are a teacher in a school, an employee in a post office, or a worker in an office building and hear sounds similar to gunshots, you should recognize that firecrackers or other pyrotechnics are not normal for your workplace, and immediately take action by implementing the ESCAPE Model presented in this book.

Case #8. **One schoolchild stated that students panicked. "Everybody just got down because they didn't know what was happening; everyone started screaming."**

Case #16. **Initially, some passengers mistook the gunshots for caps or fireworks, until a woman shouted, "He's got a gun! He's shooting**

people!" Other passengers farther away in the train did not realize a shooting had occurred until after the train stopped.[556]

Case # 25. "We thought it was just firecrackers," said one student.

Case # 26. Several students said they thought the shooting was a gag related to student-body election day. "I thought it was fake. I had never heard a gun go off," Stephani Quimby said. "It was like a movie and you were there...I knew it was real when I saw him point the gun at someone and hear a girl yell, 'Tressa!' I knew she wouldn't joke." [557]

Case #29. Some 150 teenagers gathered inside initially thought the killer was part of a skit as he began cursing and spouting anti-Baptist rhetoric.

Case #31. Waitress Kathy Pruniski heard sounds and assumed they were part of the holiday celebrations at the hotel. "Isn't that funny, they're getting a jump on New Year's," she said to some guests. "I thought they were playing some game," {one} said.

Diana Izquierdo was just about to leave with her mother when the shots started. "I thought it was firecrackers," she said.

Case #33. Bryan Snyder, shot in the left arm, said that he thought at first the attack was a prank. "It was completely unreal," Snyder said. When co-worker Carl Swanson fell to the floor, Snyder said he thought his colleague was playing around. Then two shots whizzed by Snyder, and a third tore through his upper arm. Even as he rolled to the floor, Snyder said he was convinced the man, whom he had never seen before, had shot him with a paintball gun.[558]

Case #37. Wounded student Cody Thunder said, "At first, I thought he was messing around. I thought it was a paintball gun or something.[559]

Case #44. Shawn Vidlak said the shots sounded like a nail gun, and thought it was noise from construction work. "People started screaming about gunshots," Vidlak said. "I grabbed my wife and kids. We got out of there as fast as we could."

"All of us were slightly confused because we didn't know what it was," said one mall employee about the first burst of gunfire.

Case #46. "It was just surreal," said junior Dan Sweeney. "Even when the first shot was fired I couldn't believe it was happening. It didn't seem to register with anyone."

"It didn't even sound like I thought a gun would sound like," said senior Desiree Smith. "It sounded like a cork coming out of a champagne bottle." [560]

Harold Ng said the danger didn't even register even after the firing started. "I was still in the dream state and I didn't think it was reality. It was like a video game," he said.

Case #54. A woman...was having her hair done when the gunman opened fire. "We thought it was maybe firecrackers," she said.[561]

Case #57. When Holmes re-entered the theater through the exit door, initially, few in the audience considered the masked figure a threat. He appeared to be wearing a costume, like other audience members who had dressed up for the screening. Some believed that the gunman was playing a prank, while others thought that he was part of a special effects installation set up for the film's premiere as a publicity stunt by the studio or theater management.

When Chris Ramos first saw the gunman come through the exit door, he saw objects flying in the air and thought they were fake bats.[562]

Corbin Dates said that when he saw the theater's emergency doors swing open and a man walk inside, he thought it was some kind of movie-related stunt. Even as people screamed, he thought it was part of the show.[563]

Salina Jordan was in the next theater...when she heard a series of pops. "It was so in synch we thought it was part of the movie," said Jordan. "We thought it was a special effect because they were trying to do it up big for opening night." [564]

ESCAPE: A Six Step Model for Survival

Although in the past few years there have been many articles, news accounts and blogs written about mass shootings in the United States, most of these stories have focused on the actions taken by the assailants, the types of weapons used, or the individual circumstances of the event.

After more than 30 years in law enforcement, serving in positions from police officer to Chief of Police, and having trained thousands of officers as a certified police instructor, I was interested in learning if there were specific and identifiable commonalities in the actions taken and tactics employed by those individuals who had firsthand experience as victims of mass shootings. If so, would I be able to isolate those commonalities and develop a model based on successful actions and tactics that could be used to teach others?

During the 1990s I conducted similar research into the actions taken by teachers and administrators at various school shootings which had occurred during that decade. As a result, I developed the easy-to-remember four-step RAIN Model (*Respond, Assess, Isolate* and *Notify*). This model provided educators who had a "duty to protect" with precise actions to take during a school shooting or other violent incident in order to mitigate the harm and save lives. This model has subsequently been taught to thousands of school personnel in hundreds of districts throughout the country and is featured in the book *School Safety 101: Preparing Schools and Protecting Students*_(3rd Edition).

When I began research for this book on mass shootings, I wondered if such a model was possible given the ever-changing dynamics of a mass shooting situation and the wide diversity of people and places involved. In school shootings, the locations were static in nature and the victim pool similar. Would such a model be possible when offenders ranged from mere children to senior citizens, and locations varied from shopping malls to business offices, from schools to civic buildings?

Obviously, the answer was yes, but I was amazed to discover it was a resounding YES. The actions taken, and the decisions made, by those who survived these violent incidents provided me with more than enough information to use to develop a replicable and teachable model, a model that can be taught in an age-appropriate manner to nearly everyone in any environment. I hope that throughout the country in workplaces, schools, churches, shopping malls or festivals, wherever people gather, they can apply this model and these lessons learned in order to give themselves and their loved ones a better chance at surviving a mass shooting.

NOTE: An active shooter situation is dynamic and ever-changing. Actions taken by victims must be based on the information they have at the time of the event, making the best decisions possible based on the circumstances and the totality of the information available.

The following six-step model is based on research of the actions taken by victims of previous mass shooting attacks:

Exit when possible without presenting a target;

Seek cover to protect yourself from harm;

Conceal yourself from the offenders;

Assess all alternatives;

Present a small target;

Engage, only as a last resort.

It should be noted that these steps are not sequential in nature or linear but are instead a series of fluid and conscious decisions that should be implemented as the attack unfolds and circumstances change. Assessing the situation should occur throughout the entire event and it should drive the actions taken by individuals based on their own specific set of circumstances.

For example, at the onset of the attack one might fall to the ground behind a row of seats such as in the movie theater shootings; then as the killer changes positions, one might see that protective cover is available (such as a wall in the theater) and crawl in that direction. As circumstances change, or as the shooter reloads, moves or changes his positioning or weapons, an ongoing assessment of the situation may dictate that it is time to exit the facility and put distance between the offender and his intended victims.

Additionally, some of the steps in the ESCAPE Model may be combined with the unique actions taken by mass shooting survivors, such as playing dead. For example, one may want to conceal oneself behind or under the body of another victim and play dead in order to survive the attack. This technique has been utilized on multiple occasions, most recently by some of the survivors of the Orlando nightclub massacre who concealed themselves utilizing the bodies of other fallen nightclub attendees. As noted earlier, in this case and many others, the shooter is not always aware of who he shot and loses track of victims in the chaos, providing an opportunity for survival.

E X I T

S

C

A

P

E

- ***AS SOON AS POSSIBLE WHEN SAFE TO DO SO***
- ***WITHOUT PRESENTING A TARGET FOR THE SHOOTER***
- ***WITHOUT DRAWING ATTENTION TO YOURSELF***

As the previous case illustrations made clear, on many occasions victims mistook gunfire as firecrackers, or actions by the gunman as a skit or part of a staged presentation. One assumption is that few people are familiar with the sounds of live gunfire, and therefore they assume the best and not the worst. Couple this with the fact that most people never believe that they will be in an active shooter situation, or that an event such as a mass shooting could ever happen in their community, and it is easy to see that the average citizen can't believe what they are seeing and hearing.

When confronted with a mass shooting you must take immediate action. You cannot "freeze up" or "freak out," as survivors have described their responses. You must try to remain calm, keep your wits about you, and immediately take action by exiting the location as soon as possible. **Exiting the location and thus removing yourself from the violent incident is the single most important action for surviving a mass shooting event.**

But exiting is not as simple as just jumping up from your chair and running away from the scene. You must make intelligent choices concerning escape. The autonomic response of "flight" sounds simple, but to survive an attack by an active shooter is significantly more complex.

Simply getting up and fleeing could be the worst action to take if you then present a target to the offender or draw his attention toward you. Based on the specific circumstances presented, you may have to crawl on your knees or belly or hide until the shooter's attention is diverted away from you, and then crawl or run to safety. In open spaces you may have to zigzag or vary your running pattern; when indoors, moving in short bursts from one position of cover or concealment to another may be your best option.

If you are sitting or standing by an exit and the gunman is not immediately in front of you or staring at you, exit as quickly as possible and run as far from the scene as possible. DO NOT wait and see what the gunman is going to do next or what is going to happen to others. Leave the scene immediately and do not attempt to move wounded individuals.

If you have small children, try to pick them up and run with them; otherwise drop everything else—purses, handbags, computers—so as to be as mobile as possible. While exiting, keep your hands in plain sight or over your head if ordered to do so by responding officers.

If practical, shed high heels or long coats which may impede your ability to quickly escape from the scene. Remember, *your life is at stake,* and any item that slows you down makes you more susceptible to becoming a victim.

Once you have cleared the scene, call 911 to ensure that assistance is coming. *Never assume that someone else has called 911.*

What to Report when Calling 911:

- Your specific location, with building name and office or classroom number if applicable
- Number of people at your specific location
- Injuries, with number of people injured and types of injuries (NOTE: if possible and when safe to do so, the dispatcher may provide instructions on how to care for injured until medical assistance can be provided.
- The shooter's:
    - Specific location
    - Number of shooter(s)
    - Race and gender
    - Physical features–height, weight, facial hair, glasses
    - Clothing color and style
    - Backpack or other type of bag?
    - Type of weapons (rifle/shotgun, handgun) if known
    - Do you recognize the shooter?

If you can't speak, leave the line open so the dispatcher can listen to what is taking place. This is an effective technique which has been utilized in schools to alert both students and teachers, and one that has been used for years by police officers who find themselves in dangerous situations and need to alert other officers of their need for assistance. Remember: *the single best response to an active shooter situation is to exit the location as quickly and safely as possible*. Let's look at some examples.

- ***AS SOON AS POSSIBLE WHEN SAFE TO DO SO***

Case #57. Spenser Sherman recalled, "Everybody had dropped to the floor after the first couple gunshots, and then he fired some more. And then after that, there was a pause in the gunshots. But at that point, my boyfriend was like 'This is the time, we need to go, and we need to get out of the theater right now. So we ran."

- ***WITHOUT PRESENTING A TARGET FOR THE SHOOTER***

Case #46. Desiree Smith said, "I dropped to the ground under my seat, and could see another girl down there. We just stared at each other... Then we moved all of a sudden. Everyone was army-crawling toward the back of the auditorium on the floor. As soon as I reached the door, I got halfway hunched over, and then started to run as soon as I got outside."

Case #77. About 100 people took shelter in a helicopter office at the airport. A worker turned out the lights, locked the doors and told everyone to to inside closets and other areas away from windows.

- ***WITHOUT DRAWING ATTENTION TO YOURSELF***

Case #5. When it got quiet Richard Tompkins headed for the back door. When the shooting started again toward the front of the post office, he went to the back and got a door open.

Case #57. Moviegoers dropped to the floor and crawled over one another trying to get out.

Case #61. Sam Luster hid under a desk before heading to the exit.

Case #77. Jamey Eller and her friends hit the ground when the fusillade began, then started to belly crawl, then got up and ran.

E

SEEK COVER FOR PROTECTION

C

A

P

E

Although one's initial goal may be to seek concealment or hide from the offender, an even safer course of action is to **seek cover**.

The difference between cover and concealment is that while *concealment* simply hides you, *cover* will provide you protection from bullets. Common examples of cover found in public places include parked cars, cement barriers in parking lots, brick walls, concrete support poles, or structural steel beams.

If these types of structures are not available, look for low places in the ground which might provide protection. This could be natural indentations in the ground, in drainage ditches, sewer culverts, or even laying prone on the ground alongside a cement curb in a parking lot.

Concealment such as bushes, signs or banners, or even smoke will visually screen you from the offender's line of sight but will not provide protection from bullets. Cover will stop bullets or increase the level of protection for victims seeking refuge behind these objects.

In an office or workplace, most desks do not provide cover. However, items such as file cabinets, large pieces of machinery made of steel, or other metal objects may provide protection from the attack. Structurally, most interior walls will provide a minimum of cover while exterior walls—especially those with either a brick or cinder block construction—will provide a maximum of protection from bullets of nearly any caliber. Structural support beams of either wood or steel will provide cover, as will various types of fencing and even landscape features such as retaining walls and thick trees.

Obviously, the best situation possible for a person involved in a mass shooting event who cannot safely exit the area would be to conceal himself in a place that also provides the proper amount of cover from the offender's weapons of death.

Case #5. **{An} employee escaped by locking herself in a vault where stamps are kept. Two other survivors hid in a broom closet.**

Case #29. **Some 150 teenagers gathered inside initially thought the killer was part of a skit.... They scrambled for cover as Ashbrook opened fire.**

Case #77. **Debbie Gomez and her family ran to her car and found that about 10 people were using it as a shield.**

A boulder can provide cover

Trees can provide cover

A culvert can provide cover

A brick wall or columns can provide cover

E

S

CONCEAL YOURSELF

A

P

E

- ***CONCEAL YOURSELF - HIDE FROM THE OFFENDER(S)***
- ***HIDING IN AN OPEN AREA UNDER TABLES AND CHAIRS IS NOT GOOD ENOUGH***
- ***BE CREATIVE IN FINDING PLACES TO HIDE***
- ***REMAIN HIDDEN UNTIL RESCUED BY POLICE***

If during a mass shooting or active shooter attack it is impossible to safely exit from the location or to find protective cover, the next best option is to conceal yourself from the offender. As has been noted, mass shootings are dynamic events where the shooter is actively pursuing easy targets. Since the offender often moves quickly from target to target, it is hoped that he will pass by concealed individuals, not bothering to take the time to seek them out.

If faced with a mass shooting situation, find a place to hide and then **stay hidden** until it is safe to move. Find a closet, bathroom, cabinet or storage room: whatever is available at the time, accessible at the moment, and maybe most important: out of the offender's line of sight.

In several cases individuals who ducked under a desk or table but who were still within the shooter's line of sight were systematically gunned down as the offender moved through the area.

If you find yourself in a school or office cafeteria or a food court at the mall, and your only option is to dive under the table, try to keep moving by rolling on the ground or "army-crawling" in an effort to hide from the shooter.

If you are outside and need to find concealment, consider hiding behind a row of bushes, under a pile of trash or debris, or even in a drainage ditch; these all are viable options in a life and death situation. Sometimes you may need to hide from the offender just long enough for him to lose track of you as he moves on to another target.

Under certain conditions, even areas with shadows can provide you some concealment from the shooter. This is especially true in outdoor situations where the shooter is in the bright sunlight and moving quickly between locations. Moving into the shadows may provide just enough concealment to allow you to escape harm.

Even shadows can conceal you

During such a life-and-death encounter, you may be uncomfortable for a few minutes or even longer, but you must try to remain calm and quiet until you can safely move to more protective cover or exit the situation entirely. If you are a caretaker for another person such as a young child or elderly adult, try to encourage them to be as still as silent as possible so as not to draw the attention of the shooter.

Ground cover can provide concealment

During a shooting you may only have seconds to hide. If it is possible, be creative and secrete yourself in a location where the offender will not take the time to look for you. Some ingenious places survivors have found to hide include a vault, a freezer, and even a commercial dishwasher. In each of these cases the individual survived the attack unharmed.

Once hidden, stay there until an opportunity to safely exit the scene presents itself, you can safely make it to a position that also provides cover, or you are rescued by first responders. DO NOT be impatient and try to run just because you no longer see the shooter or hear gunshots. In many cases the offender left the building and then returned to continue his assault, or simply paused to re-load his weapon, causing a lull in the action but not ending the attack.

Case #42. **Kevin Granata and Wally Grant left the locked room and went downstairs to investigate. Both were shot.**

In some instances survivors remained concealed for hours until they were sure the police were on the scene and the attack had ceased. Prematurely leaving a well-concealed place may expose one to the offender and have deadly consequences.

If your school or workplace has a lockdown procedure, it should be implemented as soon as possible in the event of an attack. A lock-down procedure may be implemented when a situation occurs that may be an imminent hazard to health, or is life threatening. It is intended to limit access and hazards by controlling and managing staff, students or other building occupants in order to increase safety and reduce possible victimization. The entire facility should have restricted access until the "All Clear" is given, or individuals are directed by emergency personnel or staff based on pre-established procedures.

Actions to minimize attention from the shooter during a lockdown:

- Proceed to a room that can be locked, close and lock all windows and doors, turn off all lights. Also block the door using whatever is available (i.e. furniture).
- Close blinds.
- Silence cell phones.
- Keep occupants calm and quiet.
- Position people out of sight and behind items that might offer additional protection (walls, desks, file cabinets, etc.).
- If there is nothing to hide behind, get everyone down on the floor and ensure that no one is visible from outside the room.
- When safe, call 911, advise the police of the incident and your location, remain in place until police or a familiar person arrives and gives the all clear using pre-established protocols.

When utilizing formal lockdown procedures, never leave your safe and secure position until you are rescued, or proper release procedures are followed. If you do not have lockdown protocols established, you should remain in a safe area until rescued by police. You must be cognizant of the fact that the shooter will not stop until his objectives have been met, unless he is engaged by law enforcement.

Before leaving your safe position, consider the risk of exposure created by opening the door. Remember that attempts to rescue people should only be made if that can be done without further endangering the persons inside a secured area.

- ***CONCEAL YOURSELF, HIDE FROM THE OFFENDER***

Case #27. Teacher Patti Nielson called emergency services as she also dialed 911 and concealed herself underneath the library's administrative counter. Brian Anderson escaped to the library where he concealed himself inside an open staff break room.

Case #49. Some of those present managed to escape to a basement, while more than a dozen hid in a closet.

Case #54. One of the employees involved locked herself in the salon's facial room and was unharmed. Another man locked himself in a bathroom but was wounded. Two doors away, the owner of a salon and her employees ran into the bathroom and locked the door.

Case #56. One man calling 911 from Café Racer said, "Someone came in and shot a bunch of people. I'm hiding in the bathroom."

Case #60. A teacher and students took refuge in a gymnasium closet. School nurse Sarah Cox hid under a desk in her office...She and school secretary Barbara Halstead then hid in a first-aid supply closet after calling 911.

First grade teacher Kaitlin Roig hid 14 students in a bathroom and barricaded the door, telling them to be completely quiet to remain safe.

Library staff Yvonne Cech and Maryann Jacob first hid 18 children in a part of the library the school used for lockdown in practice drills... [then] had the children crawl into a storage room. Cech barricaded the door with a filing cabinet.

Case #78. **Zach Poston saw a young girl hiding under a pew about to run out and kicked her back underneath.**

- ***HIDING UNDER TABLES AND CHAIRS IN OPEN AREAS IS NOT GOOD ENOUGH***

On several occasions, both in school cafeterias and in office buildings where individuals hid under desks, behind chairs or underneath tables—but in places which were still in the shooter's line of sight—the offender shot through or under the furniture, effectively "executing" those within.

Case #3. **Witness Terry Rippa said when he heard the gunshots,"We went under the table, and the guy went one, two, three, four, five down the row," Rippa said.**

Case #5. **{The gunman} bolted several doors and then systematically searched the workroom floor for workers who were cowering under tables and in cubicles. He killed three people in one work station and five in another.**

Case #10. **When someone hollered "Get down!" some realized what was happening and dived under desks to escape. There they were trapped. Pough {the gunman} started picking off those ducking for cover.**

- ***BE CREATIVE IN FINDING PLACES TO HIDE***

The best way to be creative in finding places to hide is **before an attack occurs**. In both law enforcement and military circles this tactic is referred to as "situational awareness." This involves knowing one's surroundings and making deliberate decisions beforehand on possible routes of escape, places for cover and concealment, and in some cases even sizing up possible offenders as a threat.

For the average person, situational awareness can be as simple as surveying your surroundings in an unfamiliar place for exit routes and making a mental note of places that might provide cover or concealment. One example of situational awareness which occurs hundreds of times a day for airline passengers is when the flight attendant calls travelers' attention to the escape doors, the lighted paths that lead to the exits, and the oxygen masks that will deploy under certain conditions. Whether in a restaurant, shopping mall or school, everyone should be able to practice some level of situational awareness.

Case #4. When the shooting started, {one} employee and a co-worker fled to a basement utility room, where they were joined by three female co-workers, a woman with a baby, and a man who was bleeding. They huddled in the hot basement with gunfire sounding overhead. Finally, police knocked at the door, and they opened it.

Case #5. "I heard a gunshot and hid behind some big boxes. I looked up and saw a man shooting a gun. He...then just turned in a circle shooting at random. He went towards the front lobby shooting and we ran out the back."

"I hid under my case and behind the parcel tub."

"I ran around behind some rural carrier cases trying to hide."

Two other survivors hid in a broom closet.

Tracy Sanchez and another man tried to flee through the back door, but it was locked. "We ran back and there was a storage closet nearby. We hid in there, but we couldn't lock it so we turned the light off and stayed quiet...we stayed hidden until we heard the police." [565]

Case #6. Three people huddled together unhurt in a refrigerated storeroom.

Case #11. One woman survived by hiding in a freezer. A food preparer escaped by hiding inside an industrial dishwasher.

Case #44. Shopper Jennifer Kramer said, "We hid in a pants rack towards the back of the men's department."

Case #54. One employee who locked herself in one of the salon's rooms was unharmed. A man who locked himself in a bathroom was wounded. The salon owner survived unharmed by hiding at the back of the property.

- ***REMAIN HIDDEN UNTIL RESCUED BY POLICE***

The last aspect of concealing oneself is to remain hidden until rescued by police or other first responders. If you are in a safe and secure position, wait patiently—do not move until ordered to do so. Do not respond to any voice commands until you can verify them with certainty, because an unfamiliar voice may be the shooter attempting to lure victims from their safe space. This includes responding to announcements made over intercom or public-address systems.

Schools and workplaces should have crisis response plans for concluding a lockdown without utilizing mass communications systems, since such systems can be compromised by offenders gaining access to the communications or forcing others to make false safety announcements.

Case #4. **Employee Ken Dickey and {others} fled to a basement utility room. They remained in the basement until police knocked at the door.**

Case #27. **Teacher Patti Nielson and several others locked themselves in a break room, and stayed there until they were freed, hours after the attack began.**

Case #41. **For hours after the rampage, police searched stores for shoppers and employees who were awaiting rescue.**

A storage manager, her husband and three others hid in a storage room for about 40 minutes.

Three women in an antiques shop hid under a staircase until it was safe to leave.

Case #44. **A store employee huddled in the corner of the men's clothing department with about a dozen other employees until police yelled to get out of the store.**

Another employee went with co-workers and customers into a back closet, coming out about a half-hour later when police shouted to come out with their hands up.

Case #46. **Students holed up in their dorm rooms and apartments, some staying until well after the university said the crisis was over.**

Case #60. Teacher Laura Feinstein hid with the children for about 40 minutes before law enforcement came for them.

Case #72. The police also helped eight people in another dressing room escape through an air-conditioner vent.[566]

E

S

C

ASSESS ALL ALTERNATIVES

P

E

- ***OFFENDER***
- ***VICTIM***
- ***ENVIRONMENT***

Although it may seem almost impossible, if you are exposed to a mass shooting situation it is critical to *try to remain calm and keep your wits about you* in order to properly assess the situation. A knowledgeable decision about when and how to move, or how to isolate yourself from the situation, may mean the difference between life and death. The following section presents a methodology to properly assess the situation and determine one's next move.

A simple model for assessing a situation is the Crime Triangle. This model is commonly used in law enforcement for analyzing problem solving situations and is a tool that could be applicable in mass shooting situations.

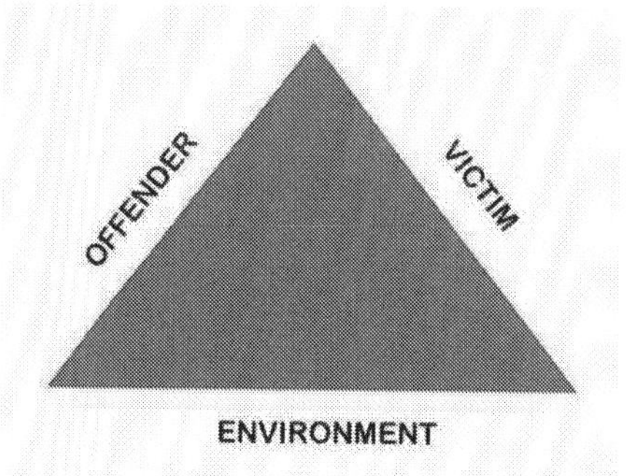

The Crime Triangle consists of three primary elements:

- **Offender** (the person who commits the crime);
- **Victim** (someone who is hurt by the actions of the offender), and
- **Environment** (the incident location, the place where the crime occurs)

During a critical incident such as a mass shooting, it is important to stay calm, to refrain from panic, and to analyze the three components of the Crime Triangle to the best of one's ability in order to make an informed decision.

For example: if you determine that the offender has not seen you and is moving away from your location, you may want to stay perfectly still until the offender has left the area. When safe to do so, you may be able to exit the building, removing yourself from harm or finding a better position of cover or concealment. Learning this step in the model is extremely important, as one must be able to quickly make some informed decisions before taking action.

Let's examine how by quickly assessing each side of the triangle we can make a more informed decision regarding our next moves during an active shooter situation.

The Crime Triangle: Offender

The first side of the triangle is the **offender**. What observations can you make about the offender which might help you to make a better decision as to the specific actions you are going to take?

One of the foremost observations is to consider what type of weapon or weapons the offender has at his disposal: does he have a handgun, shotgun or rifle? Does he have semi-automatic weapons or assault rifles? Information on the offender's weapons may provide an insight into how to respond. For example, a handgun is not nearly as accurate as a shotgun or rifle, especially at long distances (over 50 yards), and a shotgun usually has a smaller ammunition capacity than a rifle. This information may be extremely important when trying to decide if you should run and to where you should run.

Another important observation to make involves the demeanor and actions of the offender. Does he seem to be intent, almost on a mission and seeking specific targets, or just randomly shooting into a crowd?

Is the shooter aiming deliberately at a specific target?

If his actions appear to be cold and calculated as if he is seeking specific targets, you may decide to stay in a concealed position until he leaves the area. However, if he is frantic in nature and wildly spraying bullets everywhere, jumping behind the nearest cover may be the best option.

If you are in a safe place, you may want to observe the offender's clothing and his direction of movement to relay important information to responding officers. However, remember not to give up your position of safety and security to make observations. Also remember that just because an offender leaves the building or the area does not mean the incident is over or that he will not return to continue his rampage. If you are in a safe location, stay hidden until rescued by police.

The Crime Triangle: Victim

On this side of the triangle we will look at the characteristics of victim, which includes you as a participant in the event. Are you safe and secure in your current position, or do you need to move to find cover or concealment? Are you injured? If so, are you incapacitated? A twisted ankle may give you pain but still allow you to exit, whereas a gunshot wound may keep you confined to your current location. Do you need life-saving attention? If necessary, can you move to a safer location? Answers to each one of these questions may dictate your next move.

Can you assist in protecting others, such as by barricading doors or escaping out windows? If you can help protect others without exposing yourself to danger, you may want to do so. The important caveat here is *without exposing yourself to danger*. Your first duty is to remain safe at all times. If you are killed or injured, you are simply adding to the problem. This basic principle seems like common sense, yet even trained law enforcement officers must continually be reminded about officer safety.

Are you a caretaker for others such as small children or elderly adults? If so, you will want to focus on keeping them calm, reassuring them that everything will be OK, and working to keep them as safe as possible through the use of movement, cover or concealment. If you are a caretaker for others, this will have a significant impact on your decisions including when to move, where to move, and how to get there. If a member of your party is injured, especially critically, this also will factor into your assessment of the situation and, ultimately, your decision to take action.

If you can safely treat the injured, remember to continue to be aware of your surroundings at all times. Mass shootings are dynamic situations that can change in an instant. If you are knowledgeable regarding basic first aid, utilize those techniques on the most critical of injuries. In most situations you will not have access to even the most basic of first aid supplies, so be creative in identifying items to use: paper towels, napkins, even feminine hygiene products can be used to stop blood loss, and rolled-up newspapers tied with belts or shoestrings can serve as makeshift splints.

Finally, if you have a cell phone, determine whether you can quietly call or text your location to first responders so that when the incident is concluded they can locate severely injured parties in the most expeditious manner.

The Crime Triangle: Location/Environment

On this third side of the triangle, we examine the environment where these violent incidents occur. Environment certainly has played a significant role in many of the major shootings in this country. Using the Crime Triangle, we can quickly assess a situation and make appropriate decisions.

When assessing the environment, look around. Are you close to an exit or escape route, including doors or windows? Can you access a fire escape, stairwell or ladder? Can you run to safety via a hallway, or move strategically across an open area, going from object to object to provide concealment or cover?

Are you in a position that provides cover from gunfire or concealment from the offender's line of sight? Can you barricade or lock doors to protect yourself from the offender?

If not on the ground floor: can you escape out of a window or use something in the room to rappel out of the window if necessary? Are there trees to climb out onto, or bushes below that may break your fall? Can you lower yourself by hanging onto a window ledge and reducing the distance of the fall?

Though we have looked here at three separate aspects of the Crime Triangle, remember that this assessment should take only seconds. Prior time spent in assessing your surroundings, escape routes, exits, cover, or concealment will expedite this process in the event of a crisis.

Case #68. **About 10 seconds later, Meyer's statement indicates, he heard Abdulazeez pause. He yelled to Thompson, a fellow Marine that they needed run. Meyer scooped up his daughter, and the three made it out the back door unharmed.**

Case #72. **Multiple individuals who were concealing themselves behind a bar out of the shooter's line of vision noticed that he had moved away from the initial point of attack, and took the opportunity to escape out a door to safety.**

E

S

C

A

PRESENT A SMALL TARGET

E

- ***STAY LOW***
- ***CRAWL OR RUN IN A CROUCHED POSITION***

Whether you are behind cover, concealing yourself from the shooter, or deciding to flee, **try to make yourself a small target**. Make it as difficult for the shooter as possible to get off a clean shot that could seriously wound or incapacitate you.

While hiding, roll up into a ball or get into the fetal position. Try to make yourself as small a target as possible by secreting yourself in locations where it would be difficult for the shooter to see you. If you are outside, a gutter, drainage ditch or even a large curb may provide adequate cover. If you are in a school or workplace, cabinets or closets may provide a place to curl up into a ball and say hidden from an offender. Other places to "get small" may include behind heavy furniture or under certain types of tables.

The key to presenting a small target is to quickly find a place where you can hide yourself and remain patient. Don't curl up into a ball out of the view of the offender and then as soon as you stop hearing gunfire peer out, exposing your head or other portions of your body. Remember that the shooter could be reloading or simply reacquiring targets. In some situations, the offender may go outside to reload or obtain more weapons before returning and continuing on his homicidal spree.

Don't assume too soon that it's safe to emerge from hiding.

If you decide to exit the location by running, you can still present a small and much more difficult-to-hit target by running in a crouched position or hunched down. If possible and the conditions are right, you may want to present a small target by crawling from one location to another. Many moviegoers in the Aurora theater shooting presented a small target by crawling in between the rows of seats before finally deciding to exit out the nearest door.

Remember try not to call attention to yourself or draw the attention of the shooter. Running in short bursts while seeking cover or concealment may be safer then sprinting across an open area. Some research indicates that short sprints of two to three seconds don't allow an average shooter enough time to sight in on a moving target.

- ***STAY LOW***
- ***CRAWL OR RUN IN A CROUCHED POSITION***

Case #46. **Desiree Smith said, "I dropped to the ground under my seat...everyone was army-crawling toward the back of the auditorium on the floor. As soon as I reached the door, I got halfway hunched over, and then started to run as soon as I got outside."**

Case #57. **Jennifer Seeger dove into the aisle and tucked herself under a chair, and Holmes shot the person behind her. "I just laid in a ball and waited for him to go..."**

E

S

C

A

P

ENGAGE

The final step in the Six Steps to Survival Model is ENGAGE. Engaging or fighting the armed offender should occur **only as a last resort.** It is extremely rare for non-law enforcement personnel to successfully engage the shooter and actually stop the rampage. This single fact cannot be overemphasized, since all too often television news stories feature self-anointed "safety experts" who extoll the virtues of throwing pens, pencils, laptops or anything victims can get their hands on at the heavily armed and mentally focused killing machines who are bearing down on them. Unfortunately, the outcome of this ill-advised advice is all too predictable, as no one ever has successfully used these tactics to defeat a mass shooter.

Research suggests that only in the following very limited circumstances have civilians been successful in engaging the shooter:

- Engage with multiple individuals (3 or More)
- Simultaneously attacking the shooter
- While the shooter is performing some non-shooting activity (i.e. reloading weapon, changing equipment)

When a single individual engages an armed offender, the individual almost always loses. From Luigi's restaurant to Ft. Hood, Texas to Virginia Tech, people with good intentions were killed engaging the shooter. That is why ***attempting to fight back should be the last resort.***

Always keep in mind: **SAFETY FIRST**. If you are not safe, you cannot possibly help others. This is a mantra that police trainers have told their recruits for years. It's one that even casual travelers hear each time they board a plane and the flight attendants remind passengers that "in case of an emergency, place the oxygen mask over your own face before attempting to assist others."

It is heroic to want to help and stop the violence, but research clearly indicates that in nearly every documented case, the shooter has the upper hand.

There are probably numerous reasons for this result, but the most common conjecture is that an unarmed, untrained, and strategically unprepared person simply cannot overcome a well-armed homicidal maniac who is intent on killing. Mentally, the bad guy is at the location to kill, while the individual is usually just the wrong person in the wrong place at the wrong time and ill-prepared mentally, physically or emotionally to take down a sociopathic murderer.

If fighting is one's only option, then a coordinated attack by multiple individuals overwhelming the offender is much more likely to be successful. The offender only has so many weapons and can get off only so many shots before succumbing to multiple punches, kicks, stabs or other types of offensive attacks by the potential victims.

Even more successful are when the attacks coincide with the offender's preoccupation with other tasks such as reloading his weapon. This was the case in Springfield, Oregon with school shooter

Kip Kinkel, and with shooter Colin Ferguson on the Long Island Railroad train. In each case, the murderer was stopped while reloading his weapon, and attacked by multiple individuals.

- ***ENGAGE ONLY AS A LAST RESORT***

Case #1. When Red McDaniel saw that his wife had been shot, he turned toward the shooter and charged him, placing him in a bear hug. He drove King out of the church even while taking shots to the chest. McDaniel died outside the church.

Kenneth Lee Truitt also went after the shooter. A witness said that when he got to the door he leaped into the air toward King, who was just outside the door. King shot him.[567]

Case #4. Restaurant manager Neva Caine got out of her booth and went to confront the man. Huberty shot once at point-blank range and Caine died within minutes.

Case #35. Stagehand Erin Halk and security guard Jeff Thompson rushed him {the killer} from opposite sides. Thompson was shot twice in the body and once in the leg; Halk was shot in the chest, hand and leg. Both were killed.

Case #42. Matthew Joseph LaPorte, and Air Force ROTC student, was reported to have attempted to tackle Seung-Hui Cho from behind but was fatally injured in the attempt.

Case #50. Captain John Gaffaney attempted to stop Hasan, either by charging the shooter or throwing a chair at him, but was mortally wounded in the process.

Witnesses reported that civilian physician assistant Michael Cahill tried to charge Hasan with a chair before being shot and killed.

Case #54. Randy Fannin confronted the gunman, saying "Please don't do this. There's another way. Let's go outside and talk." Fannin was shot and killed.

Case #56. Gloria Leonidas {was} in a parking lot when she was confronted by Stawicki. She and the gunman were arguing, and she knocked the gun from his hand before he fatally shot her in the head and stole her car.

- ***ENGAGE ALONG WITH MULTIPLE INDIVIDUALS IF POSSIBLE***

Case #16. While {Ferguson was} reloading his third magazine, somebody yelled, "Grab him!" Three passengers tackled him and pinned him to one of the train's seats. Other passengers ran to grab his arms and legs and help hold him down.

Case #26. Student wrestler Jake Ryker tackled Kip Kinkel as he was attempting to reload his weapon. Several others quickly piled on and helped to hold the gunman until police arrived.

Case #52. As Jared Loughner stopped to reload he dropped the loaded magazine from his pocket to the sidewalk, and bystander Patricia Maisch grabbed it. Another bystander hit Loughner in the back of the head with a folding chair. The gunman was then tackled to the ground by 74-year-old retired U.S. Army Colonel Bill Badger, aided by others.

Summary

In examining the actions taken by individuals involved in mass shooting events over the past 30 years, it is possible to identify some tactics successfully utilized by survivors. Understanding that each situation is both unique in its circumstances and dynamic in its development, it is still possible to see that there are recurring patterns of behavior that can provide insight into our response to these tragic events.

In examining the commonalities in the response of individuals over the past four decades, this research has provided a significant body of knowledge beyond the traditional *"run, hide and fight"* response. Individuals who fled the scene without drawing attention to themselves, or who found cover from the hostile fire, often lived to tell their tales of survival. Others who locked or barricaded doors and found creative places to hide throughout the event frequently survived the attacks.

Unfortunately, there have been more than enough mass shootings to identify trends and make suggestions on the actions one might take if ever confronted with a mass shooting incident. The intent of this book was to examine actions and identify activities which might increase a person's chances for survival if faced with one of these horrific events.

If there is any way possible to exit, seek cover, or conceal yourself as opposed to engaging the offender: do so. Fighting back—especially if you are alone—is almost never a good idea, and should be used as a last resort only.

APPENDIX

Mass shooting Case Studies in chronological order

1. First Baptist Church, Daingerfield, Texas
   June 22, 1980
2. Bob Moore's Welding & Machine Shop, Miami, Florida
   August 20, 1982
3. Ianni's Nightclub, Dallas, Texas
   June 29, 1984
4. McDonald's Restaurant, San Ysidro, California
   July 18, 1984
5. U.S. Postal Service, Edmond, Oklahoma
   August 20, 1986
6. Shopping Center, Palm Bay, Florida
   April 23, 1987
7. Electromagnetic Systems Lab, Sunnyvale, California
   February 16, 1988
8. Cleveland Elementary School, Stockton, California
   January 17, 1989
9. Standard Gravure Printing Co., Louisville, Kentucky
   September 14, 1989
10. General Motors Acceptance Corp., Jacksonville, Florida
    June 18, 1990
11. Luby's Cafeteria, Killeen, Texas
    October 16, 1991
12. University of Iowa, Iowa City, Iowa
    November 1, 1991
13. Lindhurst High School, Olivehurst, California
    May 1, 1992

14. Office Building, San Francisco, California
July 1, 1993

15. Luigi's Restaurant, Fayetteville, North Carolina
August 6, 1993

16. Long Island Railroad, New York, New York
December 7, 1993

17. Chuck E. Cheese Restaurant, Aurora, Colorado
December 14, 1993

18. Fairchild Air Force Base, Spokane County, Washington
June 20, 1994

19. Walter Rossler Co. Office, Corpus Christi, Texas
April 3, 1995

20. Freddie's Fashion Mart, New York, New York
December 8, 1995

21. Municipal Office, Fort Lauderdale, Florida
February 9, 1996

22. R. E. Phelon Co. Plant, Aiken, South Carolina
September 15, 1997

23. Caltrans Maintenance Yard, Orange, California
December 19, 1997

24. Connecticut State Lottery Office, Newington, Connecticut
March 6, 1998

25. Westside Middle School, Jonesboro, Arkansas
March 24, 1998

26. Thurston High School, Springfield, Oregon
May 21, 1998

27. Columbine High School, Littleton, Colorado
April 20, 1999

28. Day Trading Firms, Atlanta, Georgia
July 29, 1999

29. Wedgwood Baptist Church, Fort Worth, Texas
September 15, 1999

30. Xerox Corp., Honolulu, Hawaii
November 2, 1999

31. Radisson Bay Harbor Hotel, Tampa, Florida
December 30, 1999

32. Edgewater Technology, Wakefield, Massachusetts
December 26, 2000

33. Navistar International Engine Plant, DuPage County, Illinois
February 5, 2001

34. Lockheed Martin Plant, Meridian, Mississippi
July 8, 2003

35. Damageplan Concert, Columbus, Ohio
December 8, 2004

36. Living Church of God, Brookfield, Wisconsin
March 12, 2005

37. Red Lake High School, Red Lake, Minnesota
March 21, 2005

38. Mail Processing Center, Goleta, California
January 30, 2006

39. Rave After-party, Seattle, Washington
March 25, 2006

40. Nickel Mines Amish School, Bart Township, Pennsylvania
October 2, 2006

41. Trolley Square Mall, Salt Lake City, Utah
February 12, 2007

42. Virginia Tech University, Blacksburg, Virginia
April 16, 2007

43. Apartment Building, Crandon, Wisconsin
October 7, 2007

44. Westroads Mall, Omaha, Nebraska
December 5, 2007

45. City Council Meeting, Kirkwood, Missouri
February 7, 2008

46. Northern Illinois University, DeKalb, Illinois
February 14, 2008

47. Atlantis Plastics, Henderson, Kentucky
June 25, 2008

48. Pinelake Health & Rehab Center, Carthage, North Carolina
March 29, 2009

49. American Civic Association Center, Binghamton, New York
April 3, 2009

50. Fort Hood Army Base, Fort Hood, Texas
November 5, 2009

51. Hartford Beer Distributorship, Manchester, Connecticut
August 3, 2010

52. Rep. Gabrielle Giffords Public Meeting, Tucson, Arizona
January 8, 2011

53. IHOP Restaurant, Carson City, Nevada
September 6, 2011

54. Salon Meritage, Seal Beach, California
October 12, 2011

55. Oikos University, Oakland, California
April 2, 2012

56. Café Racer, Seattle, Washington
May 30, 2012

57. Cinemark Movie Theater, Aurora, Colorado
July 20, 2012

58 Sikh Temple, Oak Creek, Wisconsin
August 5, 2012

59. Accent Signage Systems, Inc., Minneapolis, Minnesota
September 27, 2012

60. Sandy Hook Elementary School, Newtown, Connecticut
December 14, 2012

61. Santa Monica College, Santa Monica, California
June 7, 2013

62. Todel Apartments, Hialeah, Florida
July 26, 2013

63. Navy Yard, Washington, D.C.
September 16, 2013

64. Cedarville Rancheria, Alturas, California
February 20, 2014

65. Isla Vista community, Isla Vista, California
May 23, 2014

66. Marysville-Pitchuck High School, Seattle, Washington
October 24, 2014

67. Emanuel AME Church, Charleston, South Carolina
June 17, 2015

68. Chattanooga Military Facilities, Chattanooga, Tennessee
July 16, 2015

69. Umpqua Community College, Roseburg, Oregon
October 1, 2015

70. Inland Regional Center, San Bernardino, California
December 2, 2015

71. Kalamazoo Township, Kalamazoo, Michigan
February 20, 2016

72. Pulse Nightclub, Orlando, Florida
June 12, 2016

73. Protest Rally, Dallas, Texas
July 7, 2016

74. Cascade Shopping Mall, Burlington, Washington
September 23, 2016

75. Fort Lauderdale-Hollywood Airport, Fort Lauderdale, Florida
January 6, 2017

76. Awning Factory, Orlando, Florida
June 5, 2017

77. Music Festival, Las Vegas, Nevada
October 1, 2017

78. First Baptist Church, Sutherland Springs, Texas
November 5, 2017

79. Marjory Stoneman Douglas High School, Parkland, Florida
February 14, 2018

End Notes

---

[1] "The Devil and Church Violence," Safeatchurch.org. http://www.safeatchurch.org/the-devil-and-church-violence.html.

[2] "Daingerfield Shooting," Cop&Cross.org. www.copandcross.org/daingerfield-shooting.html.

[3] Luisa Yanez. "Two decades after Miami murder spree, man who stopped killer talks," The Miami Herald, October 26, 2003.

[4] "Carl Robert Brown." Wikipedia The Free Encyclopedia. 16 December 2012. http://en.wikipedia.org/wiki/Carl_Robert_Brown

[5] "Carl Robert Brown." Murderpedia The Encyclopedia of Murderers. http://murderpedia.org/male.B/b/brown-carl-robert.htm.

[6] Luisa Yanez. "Two decades after Miami murder spree, man who stopped killer talks."

[7] Gary M. Lavergne. Worse Than Death: The Dallas Nightclub Murders and the Texas Multiple Murder Law. University of North Texas Press, 2003. Online review, books.google.com/books/about/worse_than_death.html?id=Hr3OBwP-IbUC.

[8] "Abdelkrim Belachheb." Murderpedia The Encyclopedia of Murderers. http://murderpedia.org/male.B/b/belachheb.htm.

[9] "It's An Enigma. Patrons at Ianni's Bar," www.jcs-group.com/enigma/ fascinating/ patrons.html.

[10] Susana Hayward, Associated Press. "Rejected for dance, man kills woman, 5 others in nightclub," Gainesville (Florida) Sun, June 30, 1984. http://news.google.com/newspapers?nid=1320&dat=19840630&id=-3oRAAAAIBAJ&sjid=kukDAAAAIBAJ&pg=2317,4756045.

[11] "It's An Enigma."

[12] "James Oliver Huberty," biography. http://www.imdb.com/name/nm1272041/bio.

[13] "James Huberty," Murderpedia The Encyclopedia of Murderers. http://www.murderpedia.org/male.H/h/huberty-james.htm.

[14] "Gunman Kills 20 In California," Bangor Daily News, July 19, 1984. http://news.google.com/newspapers?nid=2457&dat=19840719&id=2wQ1AAAAIBAJ&sjid=F08KAAAAIBAJ&pg=3984,1331552.

[15] "James Oliver Huberty," biography.

[16] "James Huberty." Murderpedia.

[17] Amanda Covarrubias and Ernest Sander. "Haunted By The Massacre At McDonald's," The Seattle Times, July 17, 1994. http://community.seattletimes.nwsource.com/archive/?date=19940717&slug=1920774.

[18] Ibid.

[19] Amanda Covarrubias, et al. "Haunted by the Massacre at McDonald's."

[20] "James Huberty," Murderpedia.

[21] Mara Bovsun. "Mailman massacre: 14 die after Patrick Sherrill 'goes postal' in 1986 shootings," New York Daily News, August 15, 2010.

---

http://www.nydailynews.com/news/crime/mailman-massacre-14-die-patrick-sherrill-postal-1986-shootings-article-1.204101.

[22] Jacob V. Lamar, Jr. "Crazy Pat's Revenge," Time Magazine, June 24, 2001. http://www.time.com/time/magazine/article/0,9171,144859,00.html.

[23] Ibid.

[24] Ibid.

[25] "Patrick Henry Sherrill," Murderpedia The Encyclopedia of Murderers. http://murderpedia.org/male.S/s/sherrill-patrick-henry.htm.

[26] Ibid.

[27] Ibid.

[28] Ibid.

[29] Ibid.

[30] Ibid.

[31] Jacob V. Lamar, Jr. "Crazy Pat's Revenge."

[32] "Patrick Henry Sherrill," Murderpedia.

[33] Ibid.

[34] Ibid.

[35] Ibid.

[36] Barry Bearak, "6 Dead and 14 Hurt in Rampage: Florida Shooting Suspect 'Meanest Man on Block.'" Los Angeles Times, April 25, 1987. http://articles.latimes.com/1987-04-25/news/mn-990_1_palm-bay-police

[37] "William Cruse, Florida Death Row Inmate," Crime/Punishment. About.com, http://crime.about.com.od/deathrow/ig/Florida-Death-Row-Inmates/William-Cruse.htm.

[38] "Anger Remains 20 Years After Cruse's Rampage," Life on the Row. April 23, 2007. http://lifeontherow.proboards.com/index.cgi/board=ond&action=display&thread-188.

[39] Ibid.

[40] "6 Dead and 14 Hurt in Rampage."

[41] Howard Benedict, Associated Press, "6 killed, 13 injured by shopping center gunman." Kentucky New Era, April 24, 1987. http://news.google.com/newspapers?nid=266&dat=19870424&id=DOcrAAAAIBAJ&sjid=lwUGAAAAIBAJ&pg=1106,6972388.

[42] John A. Torres. "Palm Bay Killer Far From Execution 20 Years Later," The (Florida) Ledger, April 30, 2007. http://www.theledger.com/article/20070430/NEWS/704300348?p=3&tc=pg.

[43] John A. Torres. "20 years after Palm Bay massacre, killer still far from execution," The Florida Times Union, April 29, 2007. http://jacksonville.com/apnews/stories/042907/D8OQ6Q5O1.shtml.

---

[44] "Supermarket Employees Tells Her Story," Associated Press, April 25, 1987. http://www.apnewsarchive.com/1987/Supermarket-Employees-Tells-Her-Story/id-d950a475dcd5ee11a40b5abe57339080.

[45] Kenneth Ofgang. "S.C. Upholds Death Sentence in Mass Killing at Silicon Valley Firm," Los Angeles Metropolitan News-Enterprise, July 3, 2009. http://www.metnews.com/articles/2009/farl070309.htm.

[46] Dan Morain and Mark A. Stein. "Unwanted Suitor's Fixation of Woman Led to Carnage," Los Angeles Times, February 18, 1988. http://articles.latimes.com/1988-02-18/news/mn-43514_1_mr-farley-richard-farley-sunnyvale-public-safety-department.

[47] "People v. Farley, No. S024833, July 02, 2009." FindLaw. http://caselaw.findlaw.com/ca-supreme-court/1295931.html.

[48] Ibid.

[49] "Richard Wade Farley," Murderpedia The Encyclopedia of Murderers. http://www.murderpedia.org/male.F/f/farley-richard.htm.

[50] "People v. Farley," FindLaw.com.

[51] "Slaughter in a School Yard," TIME Magazine, June 24, 2001. http://www.time.com/time/magazine/article.0,9171,151105.00.html.

[52] The Associated Press. "Five Children Killed As Gunman Attacks A California School," The New York Times, January 18, 1989. http://www.nytimes.com/1989/01/18/us-five-children-killed-as-gunman-attacks-a-california-school.html.

[53] "Slaughter in a School Yard," TIME Magazine.

[54] Nelson Kempsky, Chief Deputy Attorney General, and others. "A Report to Attorney General John K. Van de Kamp on Patrick Edward Purdy and the Cleveland School Killings." October 1989. Retrieved online at http://www.schoolshooters.info/PL/Subject-Purdy_files/Purdy%20-%20official%20report.pdf.

[55] "Five Children Killed as Gunman Attacks a California School." The New York Times.

[56] The Associated Press. "Worker on Disability Leave Kills 7, Then Himself, in Printing Plant," The New York Times, September 15, 1989. http://www.nytimes.com/1989/09/15/us/worker-on-disability-leave-kills-7-then-himself-in-printing-plant.html.

[57] "Joseph Thomas Wesbecker," Murderpedia The Encyclopedia of Murderers. http://murderpedia.org/male.W/w/wesbecker-joseph.htm.

[58] "Worker on Disability Leave Kills 7, Then Himself, in Printing Plant."

[59] "James Edward Pough," Murderpedia The Encyclopedia of Murderers. http://murderpedia.org/male.P/p/pough-james-edward.htm.

[60] Ron Word. "Officials Puzzled Over Pough." The Gainesville Sun, June 24, 1990, p. 38. https://news.google.com/newspapers?nid=1320&dat=19900624&id=isFWAAAAIBAJ&sjid=PuoDAAAAIBAJ&pg=6936,8213821&hl=en.

[61] "James Edward Pough," Murderpedia.

[62] Ibid.

---

[63] Ron Word. "Massacre memories remain," The Prescott (Arizona) Courier, June 17, 1991, page 7A.

[64] Ike Flores. "Silent gunman kills 10 people, himself in two days," Mohave Dailey Miner, June 19, 1990, p. 12. http://news.google.com/newspapers?id=hD8LAAAAIBAJ&sjid=EVMDAAAAIBAJ&pg=6956,5985544&dq=pough.

[65] "Collections Darkest Day – GMAC Massacre 1990." CU Collector, June 18, 1990. http://blog.cucollector.com/hot-topics/collections-darkest-day-%E2%80%93-gmac-massacre-1990/.

[66] "James Edward Pough: GMAC Massacre," Murder by City. Crime Library, Criminal Minds & Methods. http://www.trutv.com/library/crime/photogallery/murder-by-city.html?corPhoto=12.

[67] Robert Walsh. "The Luby's Cafeteria Massacre of 1991," Crime Magazine, April 30, 2015. http://www.crimemagazine.com/lubys-cafeteria-massacre-1991.

[68] Paula Chin. "A Texas Massacre," People Magazine, November 4, 1991. Vol. 36, No. 17. www.people.com/people/archive/article/0,,20111193,00.html.

[69] Robert Walsh. "The Luby's Cafeteria Massacre of 1991."

[70] Ibid.

[71] Cindy Rugeley. "Shooting Rampage at Killeen Luby's left 24 dead," Houston Chronicle, August 11, 2001. http://www.chron.com/life/article/Shooting-rampage-at-Killeen-Luby-s-left-24-dead-2037092.php.

[72] Terri Langford. "Massacre Survivor Haunted by Dreams with PM-Massacre Anniversary," AP News Archive. October 15, 1992. http://www.apnewsarchive.com/1992/Massacre-Survivor-Haunted-by-Dreams-With-PM-Massacre-Anniversary/id-0ed7faf3fe10bff02eb9a0d941adc3c4.

[73] "George Jo Hennard," Murderpedia The Encyclopedia of Murderers. http://murderpedia.org/male.H/h/hennard-george-jo.htm.

[74] "George Jo Hennard," Murderpedia.

[75] "George Jo Hennard," Murderpedia.

[76] Terri Langford. "Man dodges massacre in dishwasher," Ocala Star-Banner, October 18, 1991. http://news.google.com/newspapers?nid= 1356&dat=19911018&id=-igxAAAAIBAJ&sjid=QQcEAAAAIBAJ&pg=2695,5940001.

[77] Paula Chin. "A Texas Massacre."

[78] Ibid.

[79] "Gang Lu," Murderpedia The Encyclopedia of Murderers. http://murderpedia.org/male.L/l/lu-gang.htm.

[80] Steven Lee Myers. "Student Opens Fire at U. of Iowa, Killing 4 Before Shooting Himself," The New York Times, November 2, 1991. http://www.nytimes.com/1991/11/02/us/student-opens-fire-at-u-of-iowa-killing-4-before-shooting-himself.html.

---

[81] Chris Earl. "University of Iowa Shootings: 20 Years Later," KCRG News, Nov. 1, 2011. www.KCRG.com/news/local/University-of-Iowa-Shootings-20-Years-Later-132997028.html.

[82] "Gang Lu," Murderpedia.

[83] Ibid.

[84] Ashley Gebb. "Supreme Court upholds Lindhurst shooter's death sentence," The Appeal Democrat. appealdemocrat.com, August 2, 2012. http://www.appeal-democrat.com/supreme-court-upholds-lindhurst-shooter-s-death-sentence/article_06361e51-88d7-565f-90d2-9a87940de251.html

[85] "Eric Christopher Houston," Murderpedia The Encyclopedia of Murderers. http://murderpedia.org/male.H/h/houston-eric.htm.

[86] Robert B. Gunnison, Ken Hoover, et al. "School Gunman Surrenders – 4 Killed in 10-Hour Ordeal," The San Francisco Chronicle, May 2, 1992. Retrieved from http://mylifeofcrime.wordpress.com/2007/05/01/lindhurst-high-school-massacre/.

[87] "Eric Christopher Houston," Murderpedia.

[88] Ibid.

[89] "Lindhurst high school shooting," Wikipedia The Free Encyclopedia. en.wikipedia.org/wiki/Lindhurst_High_School_shooting.

[90] "The Hostage Taking of Lindhurst High School Classroom C106, May 1, 1992, as told by Johnny Mills," http://www.columbine-angels.com/lindhurst_story.htm.

[91] Robert B. Gunnison, Ken Hoover, et al. "School Gunman Surrenders – 4 Killed in 10-Hour Ordeal," The San Francisco Chronicle, Ibid.

[92] "Gian Luigi Ferri," Murderpedia The Encyclopedia of Murderers. http://murderpedia.org/male.F/f/ferri-gian-luigi.htm.

[93] "Victims of Chance in Deadly Rampage." The New York Times, July 7, 1993. http://www.nytimes.com/1993/07/07/us/victims-of-chance-in-deadly-rampage.html.

[94] Jenifer Warren and Pat Morrison, "Roving Gunman Kills 8, Self in S.F. High-Rise," Los Angeles Times, July 2, 1993. http://articles.latimes.com/1993-07-02/news/mn-9236_1_law-firm.

[95] "Gian Luigi Ferri," Murderpedia.

[96] "Case 2: Kenneth Junior French," Death Penalty Curriculum. http://deathpenaltycurriculum.org/student/c/courtroom/casestudies/case2-French.htm.

[97] "Kenneth Junior French," Murderpedia The Encyclopedia of Murderers. http://murderpedia.org/male.F/f/french-kenneth-junior.htm.

[98] "(Sgt.) Kenneth Jr. French," Murderer's Profiles, Licensed to Kill. www.deepfocusproductions.com/licensed_to_kill_profiles.php.

[99] "Case 2: Kenneth Junior French," Death Penalty Curriculum.

[100] Ibid.

[101] Ibid.

---

102 "Colin Ferguson," Murderpedia The Encyclopedia of Murderers. http://murderpedia.org/male.F/f/ferguson-colin.htm.

103 "Colin Ferguson," Crime/Punishment. about.com. crime.about.com/od/murder/p/frguson.htm.

104 "Colin Ferguson (mass murderer)," Wikipedia The Free Encyclopedia. Retrieved January 14, 2013. en.wikipedia.org/wiki/Colin_Ferguson_%28mass_murderer%29.

105 Ibid.

106 Ibid.

107 Frances X. Clines. "Death on the L.I.R.R.: The Rampage, Gunman in a Train Aisle Passes Out Death," The New York Times, Dec. 9, 1993. http://www.nytimes.com/1993/12/09/nyregion/death-on-the-lirr-the-rampage-gunman-in-a-train-aisle-passes-out-death.html?src=pm.

108 "Colin Ferguson," Murderpedia.

109 Ibid.

110 Scott Kersgaard and Susan Greene. "Nathan Dunlap Death Row Case: Appeals Exhausted For Colorado Chuck E. Cheese's Killer," The Colorado Independent as reported on HuffPost Denver. February 20, 2013. http://www.huffingtonpost.com/2013/02/20/nathan-dunlap-death-row-c_n_2724716.html.

111 "Gunman Kills 4 Workers at Colorado Restaurant," The New York Times, December 16, 1993. www.nytimes.com/1993/12/16/us/gunman-kills-4-workers-at-colorado-restaurant.html.

112 Patrick Doyle and Natasha Gardner. "The Politics of Killing," The Denver Magazine, December 2008. http://www.5280.com/magazine/2008/12/politics-killing.

113 Ibid.

114 "Gunman Kills 4 Workers at Colorado Restaurant," The New York Times.

115 Patrick Doyle and Natasha Gardner. "The Politics of Killing."

116 "An Airman's Revenge: 5 Minutes of Terror," The New York Times, June 22, 1984. www.nytimes.com/1994/06/22/us/an-airman-s-revenge-5-minutes-of-terror.html.

117 "Dean A. Mellberg," Murderpedia The Encyclopedia of Murderers. http://murderpedia.org/male.M/m/mellberg-dean.htm

118 "An Airman's Revenge: 5 Minutes of Terror," The New York Times.

119 "Dean A. Mellberg," Murderpedia.

120 Dan Parker., "Victims' families see season of renewal," Corpus Christi Caller-Times, April 3, 2000. http://web.caller.com/2000/april/03/today/local_ne/4127.html.

121 "James Daniel Simpson," Murderpedia The Encyclopedia of Murderers. http://murderpedia.org/male.S/s/simpson-james-daniel.htm

122 "Dan Parker, Victims' families see season of renewal."

123 Ibid.

---

[124] Hy Drusin. "Massacre at Freddy's in Harlem: Fire Fueled by Anti-Semitism Kills 8," Jewish Post. www.jewishpost.com/archives/news/massacre-at-freddy's-in-harlem-fire-fueled-by-anti-semitism-kills-8.html.

[125] John Kifner., "8 Killed in Harlem – Arson/Gunman among dead," San Francisco Chronicle, December 9, 1995.www.sfgate.com/news/article/PAGE-ONE-8-Killed-in-Harlem-Arson-Gunman-3018812.php.

[126] Ibid.

[127] Hy Drusin. "Massacre at Freddy's in Harlem."

[128] Freida Ratliff Frisaro. "Ex-worker Kills 5, Self," February 10, 1996. The Free Library. http://www.thefreelibrary.com/EX-WORKER+KILLS+5%2c +SELF%5cFired+Florida+parks+employee+vowed+revenge.-a083904308.

[129] The Miami Herald, "Disgruntled ex-employee kills five, self," The Ocala (Florida) Star-Banner, February 10, 1996. http://news.google.com/newspapers?nid= 1356&dat=19960210&id=mzwxAAAAIBAJ&sjid=ewcEAAAAIBAJ&pg=5487,3983060.

[130] Freida Ratliff Frisaro. "Ex-worker Kills 5, Self."

[131] "Clifton McCree," Murderpedia The Encyclopedia of Murderers. http://murderpedia.org/male.M/m/mccree-clifton.htm.

[132] "Hastings Arthur Wise," www.clarkprosecutor.org/html/death/US/wise992.htm.

[133] Jeffrey Collings. "Man who killed 4 in Aiken County plant put to death," The State.com, reprinted in Murderpedia.org.[http://murderpedia.org/male.W/w1/wise-hastings.htm.

[134] Associated Press. "Factory shooter's path to execution nears end," The Augusta Chronicle, October 30, 2005. http://old.chronicle.augusta.com/ stories/2005/10/30/ met_17717.shtml.

[135] Associated Press. "S.C. plant shooter is facing execution," (Wilmington, North Carolina) Star-News, October 30, 2005. http://news.google.com/newspapers?nid=1454&dat=20051030&id=jw9PAAAAIBAJ&sjid=nx8EAAAAIBAJ&pg=6732,4242016.

[136] "Hastings Arthur Wise," clarkprosecutor.org.

[137] "Hastings Arthur Wise," Murderpedia The Encyclopedia of Murderers. http://murderpedia.org/male.W/w1/wise-hastings-photos.htm.

[138] South Carolina Bureau. "Workers describe slayings," The Augusta Chronicle, Jan. 29, 2001. http://chronicle.augusta.com/stories/2001/01/29/met_309358.shtml.

[139] South Carolina Bureau. "4 killed in Aiken County shooting; suspect caught by SWAT team," The Augusta Chronicle, September 16, 1997. http://chronicle.augusta.com/stories/1997/09/16/met_214740.shtml.

[140] "Man who killed 4 in Aiken executed," Charleston (South Carolina) The Post and Courier, November 5, 2005. http://news.google.com/newspapers?nid= 2482&dat=20051105&id=oklJAAAAIBAJ&sjid=kgkNAAAAIBAJ&pg=1362,1491357.

---

[141] South Carolina Bureau. "Survivors go on; Wise waits for execution," The Augusta Chronicle, November 4, 2005. http://chronicle.augusta.com/stories/2005/11/04/met_19187.shtml.

[142] Nick Anderson, Lee Romney, and David Haldane. "Aftermath of Killer's Fury," Los Angeles Times, Dec. 20, 1997. http://articles.latimes.com/1997/dec/20/news/mn-431.

[143] Ibid.

[144] Nick Anderson, et al. "Aftermath of Killer's Fury."

[145] Nick Anderson, David Reyes, and Esther Schrader. "4 Workers, Gunman Die in Caltrans Yard Attack," Los Angeles Times, December 19, 1997. http://articles.latimes.com/1997/dec/19/news/mn-172.

[146] Ibid.

[147] Jonathan Rabinovitz. "Rampage in Connecticut: The Overview; Connecticut Lottery Worker Kills 4 Bosses, Then Himself," The New York Times, March 07, 1998. http://www.nytimes.com/1998/03/07/nyregion/rampage-connecticut-overview-connecticut-lottery-worker-kills-4-bosses-then.html?pagewanted=all&src=pm.

[148] Strat Douthat. "Conn. Lottery Worker Kills 4, Self," AP News Archive, March 7, 1998. http://www.apnewsarchive.com/1998/Conn-Lottery-Worker-Kills-4-Self/id-ecf2612d0abe7f48227d8bfd9d39036f.

[149] Associated Press. "Lottery Victim Begged For His Life," CBS News. February 11, 2009. http://www.cbsnews.com/2100-201_162-4442.html.

[150] Jonathan Rabinovitz. "Rampage in Connecticut: the Overview."

[151] "Five die in Connecticut rampage," Lubbock (Texas) Avalanche-Journal, March 7, 1998. http://lubbockonline.com/stories/030798/LA0694.shtml.

[152] Ibid.

[153] "Lottery Victim Begged for His Life," CBS News.

[154] "Five die in Connecticut rampage," Lubbock (Texas) Avalanche-Journal.

[155] Mass Shooting Incidents in America (1984-2012) – Westside Middle School. http://www.nycrimecommission.org/initiative1-shootings.php.

[156] "Mitchell Scott Johnson," Murderpedia The Encyclopedia of Murderers. [ttp://www.murderpedia.org/male.J/j/johnson-mitchell.htm.

[157] "Andrew Douglas Golden," Murderpedia The Encyclopedia of Murderers. http://murderpedia.org/male.G/g/golden-andrew.htm.

[158] Julie Deardorff. "4 Pupils, Teacher Die In Schoolyard Ambush," Chicago Tribune, March 25, 1998. http://articles.chicagotribune.com/1998-03-25/news/9803250187_1_pupils-teacher-school-grounds.

[159] Jenny Price. "Heroes Emerge From Ark. Shooting," AP News Archive. Mar. 26, 1998. http://www.apnewsarchive.com/1998/Heroes-Emerge-From-Ark-Shooting/id-32b67db4efd8b17266988f58450ae469.

[160] Ibid.

[161] "Andrew Douglas Golden," Murderpedia.

---

[162] "Kipland P. Kinkel," Murderpedia The Encyclopedia of Murderers. http://murderpedia.org/male.K/k/kinkel-kipland.htm.

[163] Ibid.

[164] Jeff Barnard. "One Dies in School Shooting," (Alabama) Times Daily, May 21, 1998, p. 1A, 8A. http://news.google.com/newspapers?nid=1842&dat=19980521&id=TEseAAAAIBAJ&sjid=L8cEAAAAIBAJ&pg=1422,3411743.

[165] "Kip Kinkel," Wikipedia The Free Encyclopedia. en.wikipedia.org/wiki/Kip_Kinkel.

[166] Associated Press. "One Slain, 5 Critical At Oregon High School - Police Find Two More Dead At Home Of Shooter, 15," The Seattle Times, May 21, 1998. http://community.seattletimes.nwsource.com/archive/?date=19980521&slug=2751975.

[167] Jeff Barnard. "One Dies in School Shooting."

[168] "Columbine High School massacre," Wikipedia, The Free Encyclopedia. February 3, 2013. en.wikipedia.org/wiki/Columbine_High_School_massacre.

[169] Ibid.

[170] Ibid.

[171] Ibid.

[172] Ibid.

[173] Ibid.

[174] "Injured and Survivors of the Columbine High School Shooting." http://www.acolumbinesite.com/victim/injured.html.

[175] Dave Cullen, Columbine (Book). Scribd. April 6, 2009. http://www.scribd.com/doc/100886158/Columbine-Book.

[176] Associated Press. "Columbine massacre survivors push ahead," NBC News, April 20, 2009. http://www.nbcnews.com/id/30294427/#.UTVAr1eH-So.

[177] "The Columbine High School Shootings," The Criminal Mind. http://vanessawest.tripod.com/columbine-4.html.

[178] Victor Medina. "Columbine High's armed guard saved student lives," Examiner.com, December 24, 2012. http://www.examiner.com/article/fact-check-columbine-high-s-armed-guard-saved-student-lives.

[179] Dave Cullen. Columbine.

[180] Victor Medina. "Columbine High's armed guard saved student lives."

[181] Dave Cullen. Columbine.

[182] Ibid.

[183] "Columbine High School massacre," Wikipedia, The Free Encyclopedia. February 3, 2013. en.wikipedia.org/wiki/Columbine_High_School_massacre.

[184] "The Columbine High School Shootings," The Criminal Mind.

[185] Dave Cullen. Columbine.

[186] Ibid.

---

[187] Ibid.

[188] Ibid.

[189] Victor Medina. "Columbine High's armed guard saved student lives."

[190] Mark Orrin Barton," Murderpedia The Encyclopedia of Murderers. http://murderpedia.org/male.B/b/barton-mark.htm.

[191] "Portrait of a killer," Time Magazine, August 9, 1999. http://www.time.com/time/magazine/article/0,9171,991676,00.html.

[192] "Note from killer hints at revenge," CNN, July 30, 1999. http://articles.cnn.com/1999-07-30/us/9907_30_atlanta.shooting.07_1_note-death-toll-pain/3?_s=PM:US.

[193] Associated Press. "Disgruntled investor, sought in killing of 12, kills self," AP Archive, July 30, 1999. https://docs.google.com/document/d/10KNth8BgKhLheRyqBd_SBg38XZMdp4bv7rRbkKzJZxA/edit?hl=en_US.

[194] "Mark Orrin Barton," Murderpedia.

[195] Ibid.

[196] "Larry Gene Ashbrook," Murderpedia The Encyclopedia of Murderers. http://murderpedia.org/male.A/a/ashbrook-larry.htm.

[197] Ibid.

[198] "Church shooter leaves few clues as to why he went on rampage," Lubbock (Texas) Avalanche-Journal, September 17, 1999. http://lubbockonline.com/stories/091799/sta_0917990087.shtml.

[199] Ibid.

[200] Ibid.

[201] Jim Yardley. "Gunman Opens Fire at a Texas Church; Kills 7 and Himself," The New York Times, September 16, 1999. http://partners.nytimes.com/library/national/091699texas-shoot.html.

[202] Rachael Bell. "Examining Workplace Homicide – The Xerox Murders." http://web.archive.org/web/20150210050828/http://www.crimelibrary.com/notorious_murders/mass/work_homicide/5.html.

[203] Byran Koji Uyesugi," Murderpedia The Encyclopedia of Murders. http://murderpedia.org/male.U/u/uyesugi-byran.htm.

[204] Ibid.

[205] Ronen Zilberman. "Survivors emerge as key witnesses," (Honolulu) Star Bulletin, May 16, 2000. http://archives.starbulletin.com/ 2000/05/16/news/story1.html.

[206] Ibid.

[207] Steve Huettel, Linda Gibson, and Kathryn Wexler. "Gunman kills 5," St. Petersburg Times, December 31, 1999. http://www.sptimes.com/News/123199/TampaBay/Gunman_kills_5.shtml.

[208] Ibid.

---

[209] David Pedreira and Graham Brink. "Motive for targeting co-workers still unknown," St. Petersburg Times, December 31, 1999. http://www.sptimes.com/News/123199/TampaBay/Motive_for_targeting_.shtml.

[210] Mike Clary. "5 Killed, 3 Hurt in Florida Hotel Shooting," Los Angeles Times, December 31, 1999. http://articles.latimes.com/1999/dec/31/news/mn-49342.

[211] Huettel, Gibson, and Wexler. "Gunman kills 5."

[212] Ibid.

[213] J.R. Ross. "Tampa Gunman Kills 5 .Radisson Bay Harbor Employee Opens Fire in Hotel Full of New Year's Tourists," The (Lakeland, Florida) Ledger, December 31, 1999. http://news.google.com/newspapers?nid=1346&dat=19991231&id=iMtOAAAAIBAJ&sjid=Y_0DAAAAIBAJ&pg=5304,6458176.

[214] Ibid.

[215] Ibid.

[216] "Michael McDermott," Murderpedia The Encyclopedia of Murderers. http://murderpedia.org/male.M/m/mcdermott-michael.htm.

[217] Nadya Labi. "Portrait Of A Killer," Time Magazine, December 31, 2000. http://www.time.com/time/magazine/article/0,9171,93313,00.html.

[218] Ibid.

[219] Greg Sukiennik. "Officials: Rampage may have been triggered by IRS dispute," Lubbock Avalanche-Journal, December 27, 2000. http://lubbockonline.com/stories/122700/upd_075-5889.shtml.

[220] Pam Belluck. "Ex-Worker Opens Fire at Illinois Plant; 5 Are Killed," The New York Times, February 6, 2001. http://www.nytimes.com/2001/02/06/us/ex-worker-opens-fire-at-illinois-plant-5-are-killed.html.

[221] Alex Rodriguez and Matt O'Connor. "Navistar Gunman Got Past Cracks In Gun Law," Chicago Tribune, February 7, 2001.

[222] Tammy Webber. "Five dead in shooting at Illinois plant," Lubbock Avalanche-Journal, February 5, 2001. http://lubbockonline.com/stories/020501/ upd_075-7284.shtml.

[223] "5 Dead, 8 Wounded in Shooting Rampage," WDAM, July 8, 2003. http://www.wdam.com/story/1352618/5-dead-8-wounded-in-shooting-rampage.

[224] Matt Volz. "Gunman opens fire at Lockheed Martin plant in Mississippi; six dead including shooter," The Florida Times-Union, July 8, 2003. http://jacksonville.com/tu-online/apnews/stories/070803/D7S5HSKO0.html.

[225] "5 Dead, 8 Wounded in Shooting Rampage," WDAM.

[226] Ibid.

[227] "DAMAGEPLAN Shooting: What Happened The Night DIMEBAG Was Murdered?" Dimebag Darrell Tribute, December 8, 2004. Originally published in The Columbus Dispatch, January 16, 2005. http://www.dimebagdarrelltribute.com/what_happened_the_night_dimebag_died.html.

228 "Nathan Miles Gale," Murderpedia The Encyclopedia of Murderers. http://murderpedia.org/male.G/g/gale-nathan.htm.

229 Ibid.

230 Ibid.

231 "DAMAGEPLAN Shooting: What Happened The Night DIMEBAG Was Murdered?"

232 Ibid.

233 "Three Years After DIMEBAG's Murder: Missed Opportunities Abound." December 8, 2007. http://www.blabbermouth.net/news.aspx?mode=Article&newsitemID=86362.

234 "Nathan Miles Gale," Murderpedia.

235 "Dimebag Darrell," Wikipedia, the free encyclopedia. January 10, 2013. en.wikipedia.org/wiki/Dimebag_Darrell

236 "Terry Ratzmann," Wikipedia The Free Encyclopedia. February 18, 2013. http://en.wikipedia.org/wiki/Terry_Ratzmann

237 "Terry Michael Ratzmann," Murderpedia The Encyclopedia of Murderers. http://murderpedia.org/male.R/r/ratzmann-terry.htm.

238 Ibid.

239 Associated Press. "Gunman's job on line before rampage," Lubbock Avalanche-Journal, March 14, 2005. http://lubbockonline.com/stories/031405/nat_031405011.shtml.

240 Ibid.

241 Joshua Freed. "Teen who killed seven at high school believed to have acted alone," The Seattle Times, March 22, 2005. http://seattletimes.com/html/nationworld/2002215403_shoot22.html.

242 Kirk Johnson. "Survivors of High School Rampage Left With Injuries and Questions," The New York Times, March 25, 2005. http://www.nytimes.com/2005/03/25/national/25shoot.html?_r=0.

243 "Jeffrey James Weise," Murderpedia The Encyclopedia of Murderers. http://murderpedia.org/male.W/w/weise-jeffrey.htm.

244 Ibid.

245 "Teen who killed 9 claimed Nazi leanings," NBC News, March 23, 2005. [ttp://www.nbcnews.com/id/7259823/print/1/displaymode/1098

246 "Jeffrey James Weise," Murderpedia.

247 Joshua Freed. "Teen who killed seven at high school believed to have acted alone."

248 "Jeffrey James Weise," Murderpedia.

249 Kirk Johnson. "Survivors of High School Rampage Left With Injuries and Questions."

250 "Postal killer acted irrational years before attack," NBC News. February 1, 2006. http://www.nbcnews.com/id/11128315/#.UTY4q1eH-So.

---

[251] Katherine Ramsland. "Female Mass Murderers: Major Cases and Motives," crimelibrary. http://www.trutv.com/library/crime/notorious_murders/mass/female_mass_murderer/1.html.

[252] Ibid.

[253] "Jennifer San Marco," Murderpedia The Encyclopedia of Murderers. http://murderpedia.org/female.S/s/san-marco-jennifer.htm.

[254] Tim Molloy. "Shooter In Postal Rampage Had Psychological Problems," The (Owasso, Michigan) Argus-Press, February 1, 2006. http://news.google.com/newspapers?nid=1988&dat=20060201&id=eHkiAAAAIBAJ&sjid=GK0FAAAAIBAJ&pg=1331,2622008.

[255] "Postal killer acted irrational years before attack," NBC News.

[256] Associated Press. "Mayhem Stalks the Early-Morning Dregs Of An All-Night Party," KOMO News, Apr 1, 2006. http://www.komonews.com/news/archive/4181536.html.

[257] "Kyle Aaron Huff," Murderpedia The Encyclopedia of Murderers. http://murderpedia.org/male.H/h/huff-kyle.htm.

[258] "Mayhem Stalks The Early-Morning Dregs Of an All-Night Party," KOMO News.

[259] Seattle Times via Associated Press. "Gunman kills six, self in Seattle home," USA Today, March 26, 2006. http://usatoday30.usatoday.com/news/nation/2006-03-25-seattle-shooting_x.htm.

[260] Ibid.

[261] "Mayhem Stalks The Early-Morning Dregs Of An All-Night Party," KOMO News.

[262] "Kyle Aaron Huff," Murderpedia.

[263] Ibid.

[264] Ibid.

[265] Ibid.

[266] Ibid.

[267] "Amish school shooting," Wikipedia The Free Encyclopedia. January 25, 2013. en.wikipedia.org/wiki/Amish_school_shooting.

[268] Associated Press. "5th girl dies after Amish schoolhouse shooting," http://www.nbcnews.com/id/15105305/ns/us_news-crime_and_courts/t/th-girl-dies-after-amish-schoolhouse-shooting/.

[269] "Lancaster Co. School Shooting Leaves Four Dead," KYW.com, Oct. 2, 2006. http://web.archive.org/web/20061002205912/http://cbs3.com/topstories/local_story_275115123.html.

[270] "5th girl dies after Amish schoolhouse shooting."

[271] "Amish school shooting," Wikipedia.

[272] Ibid.

[273] Chris Francescani. "'Shoot Me First,' Amish Girl Said to Ask," ABC News, Oct. 5, 2006. http://abcnews.go.com/TheLaw/story?id=2531138&page=1.

---

[274] "Little Known About Utah Mall Killer," CBS News, February 11, 2009. http://www.cbsnews.com/2100-201_162-2473373.html.

[275] Ibid.

[276] Ibid.

[277] Associated Press. "Off-Duty Officer Prevented Massacre in Salt Lake City Mall Shooting Spree, Police Say," FOX News, February 14, 2007. http://www.foxnews.com/story/0,2933,251864,00.html.

[278] "Sulejman Talovic," Murderpedia The Encyclopedia of Murderers. http://murderpedia.org/male.T/t/talovic-sulejman.htm.

[279] Jennifer Dobner. "Police: Teen Shot Mall Victims at Random," The Washington Post, February 13, 2007. http://www.washingtonpost.com/wp-dyn/content/article/2007/02/13/AR2007021300105.html.

[280] "Off-Duty Officer Prevented Massacre," FOX News.

[281] "Gunman Kills Five People at Trolley Square," (Utah) KSL.com, February 13, 2007. http://www.ksl.com/?nid=148&sid=888784.

[282] Associated Press. "Gunman Kills 5 in Shooting Spree at Salt Lake City Mall Before Being Killed by Police," FOX News, February 13, 2007. http://www.foxnews.com/story/0,2933,251603,00.html.

[283] "Little Known About Utah Mall Killer," CBS News.

[284] "Seung-Hui Cho," Wikipedia The Free Encyclopedia. February 19, 2013. en.wikipedia.org/wiki/Seung-Hui_Cho.

[285] Ibid.

[286] "Worst U.S. shooting ever kills 33 on Va. campus," msnbc.com and NBC News, updated 4/17/2007. http://www.nbcnews.com/id/18134671/ns/us_news-crime_and_courts/t/worst-us-shooting.

[287] Kevin Caruso. "What Happened: The Virginia Tech Massacre," Virginia Tech Massacre.com. http://www.virginiatechmassacre.com/what-happened-virginia-tech-massacre.html.

[288] "Worst U.S. shooting ever kills 33 on Va. campus," msnbc.com and NBC News.

[289] "Kevin Granata," Wikipedia The Free Encyclopedia. en.wikipedia.org/wiki/Kevin_Granata.

[290] "Seung-Hui Cho," Murderpedia The Encyclopedia of Murderers. http://murderpedia.org/male.C/c/cho-seung-hui.htm.

[291] "Virginia Tech massacre timeline," Wikipedia The Free Encyclopedia. en.wikipedia.org/wiki/Virginia_Tech_massacre_timeline.

[292] "Liviu Librescu," Wikipedia The Free Encyclopedia. en.wikipedia.org/wiki/Liviu_Librescu.

[293] "Virginia Tech massacre," Wikipedia The Free Encyclopedia. en.wikipedia.org/wiki/Virginia_Tech_massacre

[294] Ibid.

---

[295] "Seung-Hui Cho," Murderpedia.

[296] "Virginia Tech massacre," Wikipedia.

[297] "Kevin Granata," Wikipedia. https://en.wikipedia.org/wiki/Kevin_Granata.

[298] Kate McGinty, "Horror and healing in Crandon-Killings tear at fabric of tight-knit community," (Wisconsin) Post-Crescent, October 14, 2007. http://www.postcrescent.com/article/99999999/APC0101/710140525/Horror-healing-Crandon

[299] "Tyler James Peterson," Murderpedia The Encyclopedia of Murderers. http://murderpedia.org/male.P/p/peterson-tyler.htm.

[300] Raquel Rutledge. "Shooter sought refuge with friend's family." (Milwaukee) Journal Sentinel, Oct. 9, 2007. http://www.jsonline.com/news/wisconsin/29291139.html.

[301] "People You'll See in Hell: Tyler Peterson." http://pysih.com/2007/10/07/tyler-peterson/

[302] "Nebraska Mall Shooter Broke Up With Girlfriend, Lost Job Before Massacre," FoxNews.com, December 06, 2007. http://www.foxnews.com/story/0,2933,315441,00.html.

[303] "Police: Nine killed in shooting at Omaha mall, including gunman," CNN, December 6, 2007. http://www.cnn.com/2007/US/12/05/mall.shooting/.

[304] "Nebraska Mall Shooter Broke Up With Girlfriend, Lost Job Before Massacre," FoxNews.com.

[305] "Police: Nine killed in shooting at Omaha mall, including gunman," CNN.

[306] Ibid.

[307] Kate Taylor. "I-Reporter recalls horror of Nebraska mall shootings," CNN, December 5, 2007. http://articles.cnn.com/2007-12-05/us/mall.shooting.irpt_1_westroads-mall-von-maur-jewelry-store?_s=PM:US.

[308] "Omaha Gunman's Note: "Now I'll Be Famous," CBS News, February 11, 2009. http://www.cbsnews.com/8301-201_162-3582740.html

[309] "Gunman Kills Eight, Then Himself, at Omaha Shopping Mall," Fox News, December 6, 2007. http://www.foxnews.com/story/0,2933,315342,00.html.

[310] "Charles Lee Thornton," Murderpedia The Encyclopedia of Murderers. http://murderpedia.org/male.T/t/thornton-charles.htm.

[311] Jeannette Cooperman, "The Kirkwood Shootings: Why Did Cookie Thornton Kill?" April 24, 2008. https://www.stlmag.com/Why-Did-Cookie-Thornton-Kill/

[312] "Charles Lee Thornton," Murderpedia.

[313] Ibid.

[314] Ibid.

[315] The Chicago Tribune. "Police: There were no red flags," Sun Sentinel, February 16, 2008. http://articles.sun-sentinel.com/2008-02-16/news/0802150299_1_gunman-medication-stephen-p-kazmierczak.

---

[316] Abbie Boudreau and Scott Zamost. "CNN Excusive: Secret files reveal NIU killer's past," CNN.com/crime. http://www.cnn.com/2009/CRIME/02/13/niu.shooting.investigation/.

[317] "Stephen Phillip Kazmierczak," Murderpedia The Encyclopedia of Murderers. http://murderpedia.org/male.K/k/kazmierczak.htm.

[318] U.S. Fire Administration/Technical Report Series: "Northern Illinois University Shooting." USFA-TR-167/February 2008. http://www.usfa.fema.gov/downloads/pdf/publications/tr_167.pdf.

[319] Chicago Tribune reporters, "Northern Illinois University shooting leaves 6 dead, 16 wounded." LA Times, February 14, 2008. http://www.latimes.com/news/nationworld/nation/la-na-shooting15feb15,0,3655394.story.

[320] Josh Noel, James Kimberly, and Robert Mitchum. "'I was prepared for that to be my last moment'--Attacker fired wordlessly into a mass of students," Chicago Tribune, February 15, 2008. http://articles.chicagotribune.com/2008-02-15/news/0802150151_1_gunfire-junior-shoot.

[321] Ibid.

[322] "Northern Illinois University shooting leaves 6 dead, 16 wounded," LA Times.

[323] "I was prepared for that to be my last moment," Chicago Tribune.

[324] Ibid.

[325] Robert Mitchum, Chicago Tribune, "Student: 'All I saw was the flash of shooting'." LA Times, February 14, 2008. http://www.latimes.com/news/nationworld/nation/la-na-eyewitness15feb15,0,882237.story.

[326] "Northern Illinois University shooting leaves 6 dead, 16 wounded." LA Times.

[327] Ibid.

[328] Ibid.

[329] Beth Smith. "Rampage at Atlantis Plastics ends with six dead," Evansville Courier & Press, June 26, 2008. http://archive.courierpress.com/news/rampage-at-atlantis-plastics-ends-with-six-dead-ep-448401177-325078951.html.

[330] Naomi Spencer. "US: Workplace shooting leaves six dead in Henderson, Kentucky," World Socialist Web Site, June 26, 2008. https://www.wsws.org/en/articles/2008/06/hend-j26.html

[331] Associated Press. "Police: Gunman's wife worked at care home," NBC News, March 30, 2009. http://www.nbcnews.com/id/29944382/#.UTZTiVeH-So.

[332] "Carthage nursing home shooting," Wikipedia The Free Encyclopedia. en.wikipedia.org/wiki/Carthage_nursing_home_shooting.

[333] Ibid.

[334] "Police: Gunman's wife worked at care home," NBC News.

[335] "Robert Kenneth Stewart," Murderpedia The Encyclopedia of Murderers. http://murderpedia.org/male.S/s/stewart-robert-kenneth.htm.

---

[336] Shaila Dewan. "Alleged Gunman's Wife Worked at Nursing Home," The New York Times, March 30, 2009. http://www.nytimes.com/2009/03/31/us/31shooting.html?_r=0.

[337] Michael Zennie. "Robert Stewart guilty of 2nd-degree murder, sentenced to life in prison," The Fayetteville (North Carolina) Observer, Sep. 04, 2011. http://www.fayobserver.com/articles/2011/09/03/1120314?sac=Home.

[338] "Binghamton struggles to understand why gunman killed 13," CNN, April 5, 2009. http://www.cnn.com/2009/CRIME/04/04/binghamton.shooting/index.html.

[339] Joe Kemp, Mathew Lysiak, and Corky Siemaszko. "Who is Jiverly Voong aka Jiverly Wong?" New York Daily News, April 4, 2009. www.nydailynews.com/news/jiverly-voong-aka-jiverly-wong-conflicting-picture-binghamton-gunman-emerges-article-1.359248?

[340] "Binghamton shootings." Wikipedia The Free Encyclopedia. February 3, 2013. en.wikipedia.org/wiki/Binghamton_shootings.

[341] "Jiverly Antares Wong," Murderpedia The Encyclopedia of Murderers. http://murderpedia.org/male.W/w/wong-jiverly.htm.

[342] Ibid.

[343] Ibid.

[344] "Binghamton struggles to understand why gunman killed 13," CNN.

[345] Joe Kemp and Matthew Lysiak. "Survivor of Binghamton massacre tried in vain to save his wife," New York Daily News. April 6, 2009. http://www.nydailynews.com/news/survivor-binghamton-massacre-vain-save-wife-article-1.360199.

[346] The Associated Press. "Fort Hood Shooter Nidal Hasan Sentenced to Death," CBC News World, August 28, 2013. http://www.cbc.ca/news/world/fort-hood-shooter-nidal-hasan-sentenced-to-death-1.1391606?cmp=rss.

[347] Mike Baker and Brett Blackledge. "Ft. Hood UPDATES: New Clues in Military Base Shooting," Huff Post, 11/06/09. http://www.huffingtonpost.com/2009/11/06/ft-hood-updates-new-clues_n_348157.html.

[348] Nidal Malik Hasan," Murderpedia The Encyclopedia of Murderers. http://murderpedia.org/male.H/h/hasan-nidal.htm.

[349] Jeremy Schwartz. "Witnesses in Fort Hood shooting hearing say Hasan returned to shoot same victims over and over," (Austin) Statesman.com, Oct. 15, 2010. http://www.statesman.com/news/news/state-regional/witnesses-in-fort-hood-shooting-hearing-say-hasan-/nRykN/.

[350] "Nidal Malik Hasan," Murderpedia.

[351] Brad Knickerbocker. "Alleged Fort Hood shooter Maj. Nidal Hasan faces March 2012 trial," The Christian Science Monitor, July 20, 2011. http://www.csmonitor.com/USA/Military/2011/0720/Alleged-Fort-Hood-shooter-Maj.-Nidal-Hasan-faces-March-2012-trial.

---

352 Jay Root. "Officer Describes Firefight That Downed Hasan," NBC DFW, Nov 7, 2009. http://www.nbcdfw.com/news/local/Officer-Describes-Firefight-That-Downed-Hasan-69488762.html.

353 "Nidal Malik Hasan," Murderpedia.

354 Charley Keyes. "Despite alarming detail, Fort Hood shooting case still mysterious," CNN. November 17, 2010. http://www.cnn.com/2010/CRIME/11/17/texas.fort.hood.case/index.html.

355 Charley Keyes. "Witnesses recount bloody scenes at Fort Hood hearing," CNN. October 20, 2010. http://www.cnn.com/2010/CRIME/10/19/texas.fort.hood.shootings/index.html.

356 "Omar S. Thornton," Murderpedia The Encyclopedia of Murderers. http://murderpedia.org/male.T/t/thornton-omar.htm.

357 Ray Rivera and Liz Robbins. "Troubles Preceded Connecticut Workplace Killing," The New York Times, August 3, 2010. http://www.nytimes.com/2010/08/04/nyregion/04shooting.html?pagewanted=all.

358 "Jared Lee Loughner," Murderpedia The Encyclopedia of Murderers. http://murderpedia.org/male.L/l/loughner-jared.htm.

359 Ibid.

360 "Giffords Gunman Jared Loughner Jailed For Life," Sky News, November 9, 2012. [http://news.sky.com/story/1008950/giffords-gunman-jared-loughner-jailed-for-life]

361 "2011 Tucson shooting," Wikipedia The Free Encyclopedia. February 15, 2013. [en.wikipedia.org/wiki/2011_Tucson_shooting]

362 "Jared Lee Loughner," Murderpedia.

363 "2011 Tucson shooting," Wikipedia.

364 "Eduardo Sencion," Murderpedia The Encyclopedia of Murderers. http://murderpedia.org/male.S/s/sencion-eduardo.htm.

365 "IHOP shooting death toll rises to 5," CBS News, September 7, 2011. http://www.cbsnews.com/2100-201_162-20102475-2.html.

366 Steve Keegan. "Four dead, nine wounded in Nevada shooting," Barrie (Ontario) Examiner, September 6, 2011. http://www.thebarrieexaminer.com/2011/09/06/four-dead-nine-wounded-in-nevada-shooting-5.

367 Adolfo Flores. "Seal Beach mass shooting suspect Scott Dekraii now a convicted killer," http://www.latimes.com/local/la-me-0503-seal-beach-killer-20140503-story.html.

368 Paul Bentley, David Gardner, and Mark Duell. "'He lived for his son': Gunman 'shot dead eight in beauty salon massacre to get back at hairdresser wife over custody battle'", The (U.K.) Daily Mail, October 13, 2011. http://www.dailymail.co.uk/news/article-2048470/Seal-Beach-shooting-8-killed-Scott-Dekraai-targets-ex-wife-Orange-county-hair-salon.html.

---

[369] "DA seeks death penalty in salon murders," Sun Newspapers, October 14, 2011. http://www.sunnews.org/latest-news/da-seeks-death-penalty-in-salon-murders/.

[370] Associated Press. "Some say Calif. gunman was ex-husband," CBSnews.com, October 13, 2011. http://www.cbsnews.com/2100-201_162-20119641.html.

[371] "Scott Evans Dekraii," Murderpedia The Encyclopedia of Murderers. http://murderpedia.org/male.D/d/dekraai-scott.htm.

[372] "8 killed in Southern California salon shooting," CNS News, October 12, 2011. http://cnsnews.com/8-killed-southern-california-salon-shooting-2.

[373] "Some say Calif. gunman was ex-husband," CBSnews.com.

[374] "Scott Evans Dekraii," Murderpedia.

[375] Terry Collins. "One Goh, Oikos University Shooting Suspect, Deemed Unfit For Trial," (San Francisco) The Huffington Post, January 7, 2013. http://www.huffingtonpost.com/2013/01/07/one-goh-oikos_n_2428444.html.

[376] Ruggiero, Angela. "Oikos nursing school massacre shooter One God sentenced to life in prison," The Mercury News, July 14, 2017. https://www.mercurynews.com/2017/07/14/oikos-nursing-school-massacre-suspect-one-goh-to-face-life-in-prison/

[377] Matthias Gafni et al. "Oakland university shooting: Accused Oikos University shooter One Goh was 'troubled,' 'angry,' said those who knew him," Oakland Tribune, April 3, 2012. http://www.insidebayarea.com/oakland-tribune/ci_20314383/oakland-school-rampage-suspect-sought-revenge-against-administrator.

[378] David Gardner, Rob Cooper, and Meghan Keneally. "Oakland massacre gunman's boasts about violence revealed as relatives mourn students shot 'because they didn't do what he said'", The Daily Mail, April 2, 2012. http://www.dailymail.co.uk/news/article-2124173/Oakland-shooting-Gunman-One-Gohs-boasts-massacre-Oikos-University-California-revealed.html.

[379] Ibid.

[380]Gillian Mohney. "Oikos University Shooting: Suspect, One L. Goh, Detained; At Least 7 Dead," ABC News. April 2, 2012. http://abcnews.go.com/US/oakland-shooting-dead-oikos-university-suspect-idd-goh/story?id=16056854.

[381] Ibid.

[382] Mary Slosson and Lalit K Jha. "Indian among the seven killed in Oakland shooting incident," DNA India, Apr 3, 2012. http://www.dnaindia.com/world/report_indian-among-the-seven-killed-in-oakland-shooting-incident_1670789.

[383] Jim Vojtech, Alyssa Newcomb, and Michael S. James. "Seattle Café Shooter Kills 5, and Himself After Citywide Manhunt," ABC News, May 31, 2012. http://abcnews.go.com/US/ian-stawicki-seattle-cafe-racer-shooter-kills-shoots-citywide/story?id=16463885&singlePage=true#.UVnlgRzvu8c.

[384] "Police laud 'hero' in Seattle shootings," Fox News, June 1, 2012. http://www.foxnews.com/us/2012/06/01/police-laud-hero-in-seattle-shootings/.

[385] Ibid.

---

386 "Police: 'Hero' saved several Seattle cafe patrons as gunman opened fire," CNN, May 31, 2012. http://www.cnn.com/2012/05/31/us/washington-cafe-shooting.

387 "Police laud 'hero' in Seattle shootings," Fox News.

388 Gene Johnson and Shannon Dininny. "Police laud 'hero' in Seattle shootings." Columbian.com, June 1, 2012. http://www.columbian.com/news/2012/jun/01/police-laud-hero-seattle-shootings/?print.

389 Casey McNerthney. "Police credit homeless felon for helping at tragic shooting," KOMO News, June 1, 2012.[http://www.komonews.com/news/local/Police-credit-homeless-felon-for-helping-at-tragic-shooting-156495735.html.

390 "Seattle shootings: day of horror, grief in a shaken city," The Seattle Times, May 30, 2012. http://seattletimes.com/html/localnews/2018316552_roosevelt31m.html.

391 Ann O'Neill. "Theater shooter Holmes gets 12 life sentences, plus 3,318 years," CNN.com, August 27, 2015. http://www.cnn.com/2015/08/26/us/james-holmes-aurora-massacre-sentencing/.

392 Michael Muskal. "Questions, but few answers, in Colorado shooting; 12 dead, dozens hurt," Los Angeles Times, July 20, 2012. http://articles.latimes.com/2012/jul/20/nation/la-na-nn-colorado-shooting-update-batman-20120720.

393 "2012 Aurora shooting," Wikipedia The Free Encyclopedia. February 24, 2013. en.wikipedia.org/wiki/2012_Aurora_shooting.

394 "Aurora Colorado Shooting Tragedy From a Local's Perspective," Empower Network, August 3, 2012. http://www.empowernetwork.com/freedombacknow/blog/aurora-colorado-shooting-tradegy-from-a-local/.

395 "2012 Aurora shooting," Wikipedia.

396 Ibid.

397 Jennifer Brown. "12 shot dead, 58 wounded in Aurora movie theater during Batman premiere," The Denver Post, July 21, 2012. http://www.denverpost.com/news/ci_21124893/12-shot-dead-58-wounded-aurora-movie-theater.

398 Ryan Parker, Joey Bunch, Kurtis Lee, John Ingold, Jordan Steffen, and Jennifer Brown. "Family identifies 27-year-old victim of Aurora theater shooting," The Denver Post, July 20, 2012. http://www.denverpost.com/breakingnews/ci_21118201/unknown-number-people-shot-at-aurora-movie-theater.

399 Sari Horwitz and Debbi Wilgoren. "Police say Colorado shooting suspect James Holmes had 2 pistols, assault rifle, shotgun," The Washington Post, July 20, 2012. http://failover.washingtonpost.com/world/national-security/colorado-shooter-identified-as-james-holmes-24/2012/07/20/gJQAWkdrxW_story_2.html.

400 "Aurora witnesses describe shooter's entrance, chaos," CBS News, July 20, 2012. http://www.cbsnews.com/8301-505263_162-57476424/aurora-witnesses-describe-shooters-entrance-chaos/.

---

[401] Ryan Parker et al. "Family identifies 27-year-old victim of Aurora theater shooting."

[402] Jennifer Brown "12 shot dead, 58 wounded."

[403] Miguel Bustillo, Shelly Banjo, and Tamara Audi. "Theater Rampage Jolts Nation," The Wall Street Journal, July 21, 2012. http://online.wsj.com/article/SB10000872396390444464304577538292604705890.html.

[404] Ed Pilkington and Matt Williams. "Colorado theater shooting: 12 shot dead during The Dark Knight Rises screening," The (U.K.) Guardian, July 20, 2012. http://www.guardian.co.uk/world/2012/jul/20/colorado-theater-shooting-dark-knight.

[405] "Shooting at Sikh temple in Wisconsin leaves at least 7 dead, including gunman," FoxNews.com, August 6, 2012. http://www.foxnews.com/us/2012/08/05/possible-injuries-after-shooting-at-sikh-temple-in-wisconsin/.

[406] Brian Louis, Henry Goldman and Chris Christoff. "Wisconsin Sikh Shooting Suspect Formed Skinhead Bands," Bloomberg News, August 7, 2012. http://www.bloomberg.com/news/print/2012-08-06/wisconsin-sikh-shooting-probed-by-fbi-as-domestic-terror.html.

[407] "Shooting at Sikh temple in Wisconsin leaves at least 7 dead, including gunman."

[408] Ted Rowlands. "Sikhs repair, reclaim temple after rampage," CNN.com, August 10, 2012. http://www.cnn.com/2012/08/09/justice/wisconsin-temple-shooting/index.html.

[409] Brian Louis, et al. "Wisconsin Sikh Shooting Suspect Formed Skinhead Bands."

[410] Matt McKinney. "Accent Signage Systems shooting: First victims fought for their lives," (Minneapolis) Star Tribune, October 2, 2012. http://www.startribune.com/loacl/minneapolis/html?refer=y.

[411] Jennifer Bjorhus and Todd Nelson. "Accent rebuilds after Minneapolis workplace rampage," (Minneapolis) Star Tribune, April 5, 2013. http://www.startribune.com/accent-rebuilds-after-minneapolis-workplace-rampage/200746171/.

[412] "Illegal Gun Crime - Mass Shooting Incidents in America (1984-2012), Sandy Hook Elementary School," Citizens Crime Commission of New York City. http://www.nycrimecommission.org/initiative1-shootings.php.

[413] John Christoffersen. "Newtown Shooting Motive Remains Unclear Following Search Warrant Revelations On Adam Lanza," Huff Post CRIME, March 29, 2013. http://www.huffingtonpost.com/2013/03/29/newtown-shooting-motive_n_2978093.html.

[414] M. Alex Johnson and Becky Bratu. "Police: Second person injured in Connecticut school shooting survived," NBCnews.com, December 17, 2012. http://usnews.nbcnews.com/_news/2012/12/17/15969867-police-second-person-injured-in-connecticut-school-shooting-survived?lite.

---

415 "Sandy Hook Elementary School shooting," Wikipedia The Free Encyclopedia. February 24, 2013. https://en.wikipedia.org/wiki/Sandy_Hook_Elementary_School_shooting.

416 John Christoffersen, "Newtown Shooting Motive Remains Unclear."

417 Ibid.

418 Ibid.

419 "New York Daily News 2012 Person of the Year winner: The brave faculty of Sandy Hook Elementary School," New York Daily News, December 30, 2012, updated December 31, 2012. http://www.nydailynews.com/new-york/new-york-daily-news-2012-person-year-winner-brave-faculty-sandy-hook-elementary-school-article-1.1230018?pgno=2.

420 Christine Roberts. "Teacher's words of comfort to class during Newtown rampage: 'I love you all very much ... it's going to be OK.", New York Daily News, December 18, 2012. http://www.nydailynews.com/news/national/sandy-hook-teacher-speaks-ordeal-article-1.1222727.

421 "Sandy Hook Elementary School shooting," Wikipedia.

422 Ibid.

423 "Teacher died fighting for her students," The Houston Chronicle, December 15, 2012. http://www.chron.com/news/nation-world/nation/article/Teacher-died-fighting-for-her-students-4121117.php.

424 Ibid.

425 Eileen FitzGerald. "Principal, school psychologist ran to help," (Danbury, Connecticut) News Times, December 14, 2012. http://www.newstimes.com/news/article/Principal-school-psychologist-ran-to-help-4119969.php.

426 Lia Eustachewich. "Connecticut victims ID'd as police uncover 'very good evidence' of shooter's motives," New York Post, December 15, 2012. http://www.nypost.com/p/news/local/connecticut_victims_shooter_motives_dM0QIY1PQjY7PxV1pebrJK.

427 "Sandy Hook Elementary School shooting," Wikipedia.

428 Billy Nilles. "Sandy Hook Teacher Who Died Shielding Special Needs Boy, 6, Like 'Jesus'." Hollywood Life, December 20, 2012. http://hollywoodlife.com/2012/12/20/sandy-hook-special-ed-teacher-funeral-anne-marie-murphy/.

429 "Sandy Hook Elementary School shooting," Wikipedia.

430 "Sandy Hook Classroom Survivor Played Dead," ABC News, Dec 17, 2012. http://abcnews.go.com/blogs/headlines/2012/12/sandy-hook-classroom-survivor-played-dead/.

431 "Gunman at college planned his rampage," Los Angeles Times, June 18, 2013. http;//www.sfgate.com/crime/article/Gunman-at-college-planned-his-rampage-4589484.php.

---

[432] Pamela Engel, provided by Business Insider. "The Santa Monica Shooter Had a Troubled Past," June 11, 2013. http://www.sfgate.com/default/article/The-Santa-Monica-Shooter-Had-A-Troubled-Past-4593861.php.

[433] The Associated Press. "Santa Monica Shooting Victims: Background of Those Killed in Rampage," June 10, 2013. http://huffingtonpost.com/2013/06/10/santa-monica-shooting-victims_n_3414710.html.

[434] Ibid.

[435] Sgt. Richard Lewis. Santa Monica Police Department Press Release. June 13, 2013.

[436] Michael Winter and William Cummings. "Police: Santa Monica gunman acted alone, killing 4," USA Today, June 8, 2013. http://origin.ksdk.com/news/world/article/383949/28/Police-Santa-Monica-gunman-acted-alone-killing-4.

[437] Ibid.

[438] Michael Martinez, Susan Candiotti and Stan Wilson. "Source: Santa Monica gunman previously hospitalized for mental health," CNN, June 8, 2013. http://www.cnn.com/2013/06/08/us/california-college-gunman/index.html.

[439] Tami Abdollah. "Chief says Santa Monica killings were premeditated," SFGate.com, June 8, 2013. [http://www.sfgate.com/default /article/Chief-says-Santa-Monica-killings-were-premeditated-4589023.php]

[440] The Associated Press. "Santa Monica Shooting Victims: Background of Those Killed in Rampage," Huffpost, June 10, 2013. http://www.huffingtonpost.com/2013/06/10/santa-monica-shooting-victims_n_3414710.html.

[441] Patricia Mazzel, Maria Perez and Melissa Sanchez. "Hialeah killer showed signs of trouble before mass shooting," Miami Herald, August 8, 2013. http://www.miamiherald.com/2013/08/03/3539629/hialeah-killer-showed-signs-of.html.

[442] Ibid.

[443] Benjamin Mueller. "Gunman in Florida apartment shooting lived in building, started fire," Los Angeles Times. July 27, 2013. http://www.latimes.com/nation/nationnow/la-na-nn-florida-gunman-hialeah-20130727-story.html.

[444] Joey Flechas, Glenda Ortega, Charles Rabin and Julie K. Brown. "Hialeah shootings: Seven, including gunman, dead after standoff," Miami Herald, posted August 2, 2013. http://www.miamiherald.com/2013/07/27/3525365/seven-dead-after-standoff-shootings.html.

[445] Zachary Fagenson. "Motive a mystery in Miami area mass shooting," Reuters News Service, Miami, July 28, 2013. [http://www.reuters.com/ assets/print?aid= USBRE96Q06G20130729]

[446] Patricia Mazzel et al. "Hialeah killer showed signs of trouble."

[447] Joey Flechas et al. "Hialeah shootings: Seven, including gunman, dead after standoff."

[448] Michael Pearson, Ed Payne and Pamela Brown. "Navy Yard shooting survivor: 'I got lucky'." CNN.com. www.cnn.com/2013/09/18/us/navy-yard-shooting-main/index.html.

---

[449] Ibid.

[450] Eric Tucker. "Gunman didn't target victims," Dallas Morning News, September 26, 2013. p. 4A.

[451] Tara McKelvey. "Washington Navy Yard shooting: Survivors' ordeals." BBC News US & Canada, September 16, 2013. http://www.bbc.co.us/news/world-us-canada-24119601.

[452] Jim Avila and Serena Marshall. "'Anybody He Saw, He Shot': DC Navy Yard Shooting Survivor Says He Watched Aaron Alexis Kill Friends, Coworkers," ABCNews.Go.com, September 18, 2013. http://abcnews.go.com/US/dc-navy-yard-shooting-survivor-watched-aaron-alexis/story?id=20299371

[453] Corky Siemaszko. "'I felt him breathe': Survivor of Washington Navy Yard shooting talks about trying to save life of Vishnu Pandit, a co-worker killed during massacre," New York Daily News, September 20, 2013. http://www.nydailynews.com/news/national/survivor-recalls-save-washington-navy-yard-victim-article-1.1462479.4

[454] "Cherie Lash-Rhoades Sentencing." April 10, 2017. KRCR-TV. http://krcrtv.com/news/local/cherie-lash-rhoades-sentencing

[455] Phil Willon. "Tribal shooting suspect was known for her temper," Los Angeles Times, February 22, 2014. http://articles.latimes.com/2014/feb/22/local/la-me-tribal-slayings-20140223.

[456] Ian McDonald. "Husband Recounts Chilling Lead-Up to Alturas Shooting." Fox40.com, March 30, 2014. http://fox40.com/2014/03/19/husband-recounts-chilling-lead-up-to-alturas-shooting/.

[457] KRCR Staff. "Alleged mass shooter to stand trial for murder in tribal dispute," KRCR News, May 13, 2016. http://krcrtv.com/archive/alleged-mass-shooter-to-stand-trial-for-murder-in-tribal-dispute

[458] Ibid.

[459] Alan Duke. "Timeline to 'Retribution': Isla Vista attacks planned over years," CNN, May 27, 2014, http://www.cnn.com/2014/05/26/justice/california-elliot-rodger-timeline/.

[460] "2014 Isla Vista Killings," Wikipedia, https://en.wikipedia.org/wiki/2014_Isla_Vista_killings.

[461] Victoria Sanchez. "Shooting Survivor Sierra Swartz Shares Story," KEYT.com, May 26, 2014.

[462] Chelsea J. Carter. "Washington state school shooting: 'Run, get out of here.' "CNN. October 25, 2014, http://www.cnn.com/2014/10/24/us/washington-school-shooting/index.html.

[463] Ibid.

[464] Ryan Parry. "Best friend of Washington high school shooter survived by stifling urge to scream and PLAYING DEAD." Dailymail.com. http://www.dailymail.co.uk/news/article-2810583/Best-friend-Washington-high-

school-shooter-survived-stifling-urge-scream-PLAYING-DEAD-cafeteria-floor-bullet-tore-jaw.html.

[465] Blinder, Alan and Sack, Kevin. "Dylann Roof is Sentenced to Death in Charleston Church Massacre," The New York Times, January 10, 2017. https://www.nytimes.com/2017/01/10/us/dylann-roof-trial-charleston.html

[466] Jennifer Berry Hawes and Doug Pardue. "In an hour, a church changes forever," The Post and Courier, June 19, 2015, http://www.postandcourier.com/article/20150619/PC16/150619306.

[467] Katie Zavadski, "Everything Known About Charleston Church Shooting Suspect Dylann Roof." June 20, 2015, https://www.thedailybeast.com/everything-known-about-charleston-church-shooting-suspect-dylann-roof

[468] Jennifer Berry Hawes and Doug Pardue. "In an hour, a church changes forever."

[469] Brian Ross, Doug Lantz, and James Gordon Meek, "Chattanooga Shooter Researched Religious Justification for Violence; Official," ABC News, July 20, 2015, http://abcnews.go.com/US/chattanooga-shooting-fbi-recovers-gunmans-disturbing-diary/story?id=32558310.

[470] Ibid.

[471] "2015 Chattanooga shootings," Wikipedia, https://en.wikipedia.org/wiki/2015_Chattanooga_shootings#cite_note-ShooterDiary-9.

[472] Brian Ross, et al. "Chattanooga Shooter Researched Religious Justification."

[473] Gina Harkins. "Chattanooga shooting investigation: Marine shielded his daughter from terrorist's rampage." Marine Corps Times, Sept. 25, 2015, https://www.marinecorpstimes.com/story/military/2015/09/25/chattanooga-shooting-investigation-marine-recruiter-shielded-daughter-from-muhammad-youssef-abdulazeez-rampage/72586592/.

[474] Ibid.

[475] Ibid.

[476] Mary Beth McDade, Eric Spillman and Erin Mayes. "Oregon Gunman Was Enrolled in Class Where He Opened Fire, Authorities Say," CNN, October 1, 2015, http://ktla.com/2015/10/01/umpqua-community-college-shooter-targeted-christians-father-of-oregon-shooting-victim-says/.

[477] Jack Healy, Mike McIntire and Julie Turkewitz. "Oregon killer and mother bonded over guns," The Seattle Times, October 5, 2015. http://www.seattletimes.com/nation-world/nation/oregon-killer-and-mother-had-close-bond-with-guns/.

[478] Eric M. Johnson and Emily Flitter. "Oregon gunman slipped into isolation after California move." Yahoo! News, October 7, 2015, https://www.yahoo.com/news/oregon-gunman-slipped-isolation-california-move-223311849.html.

[479] Michael E. Miller and Yanan Wang, "Oregon shooter left behind online portrait of a lonely youth with a grudge against religion," The Washington Post, October 2, 2015,

https://www.washingtonpost.com/news/morning-mix/wp/2015/10/02/ore-shooter-left-behind-online-portrait-of-a-lonely-youth-with-a-grudge-against-religion/.

480 Mary Beth McDade, et al. "Oregon Gunman Was Enrolled in Class."

481 Laura Gunderson. "Oregon school shooting: Umpqua shooter on academic probation," The Oregonian, October 23, 2015, http://www.oregonlive.com/pacific-northwest-news/index.ssf/2015/10/oregon_school_shooting_umpqua.html.

482 Kenneth R. Rosen. "Survivor of Oregon Shooting Writes About Encounter With an Emotionless Gunman." The New York Times. Oct. 17, 2015, http://www.nytimes.com/2015/10/18/us/survivor-of-oregon-shooting-writes-about-encounter-with-an-emotionless-gunman.html?smid=pl-share&_r=0.

483 The Associated Press. "At least 10 dead in shooting at Oregon community college." The Dallas Morning News, October 2, 2015, http://www.dallasnews.com/news/local-news/20151001-officials-report-active-shooter-at-oregon-community-college.ece.

484 Amanda Lee Myers and Justin Pritchard. "14 dead, 17 wounded in California shooting; 2 suspects dead," ABC News, December 2, 2015, http://www.businessinsider.com/ap-14-dead-17-wounded-in-california-shooting-2-suspects-dead-2015-12.

485 "San Bernardino Shooters Had More Than 6,000 Rounds of Ammo, Police Say," WTNH News, December 4, 2015, http://wtnh.com/2015/12/03/san-bernardino-shooters-had-more-than-6000-rounds-of-ammo-police-say/.

486 Miguel Almaguer and Corky Siemaszko. " 'Why Won't He Stop Shooting?' San Bernardino Terror Attack Survivors Speak," NBC News, December 7, 2015, http://www.nbcnews.com/storyline/san-bernardino-shooting/san-bernardino-shooting-survivors-speak-n475756.

487 "San Bernardino shooting victims: who they were," Los Angeles Times, December 17, 2015, http://www.latimes.com/local/lanow/.

488 Amanda Lee Myers and Justin Pritchard. "14 dead, 17 wounded."

489 Brad Devereaux. "Pain, memories remain 2 years after Kalamazoo mass shooting." Kalamazoo News, February 20, 2018. http://www.mlive.com/news/kalamazoo/index.ssf/2018/02/family_of_kalamazoo_mass_shoot_1.html

490 Ryan Felton. "Kalamazoo shooter saw 'devil' on Uber app and blames visions for killing spree," The Guardian, March 14, 2016, https://www.theguardian.com/us-news/2016/mar/14/kalamazoo-shooter-jason-dalton-uber-iphone-takes-over-body.

491 Shandra Martinez. "Gun shop owner describes purchase by Kalamazoo mass murder suspect," MLive.com, February 23, 2016, http://www.mlive.com/business/west-michigan/index.ssf/2016/02/gun_owner_describe_ purchase_by.html.

492 Katrease Stafford. "After Kalamazoo shootings, the big question: Why?" USA Today Network, February 22, 2016, http://www.usatoday.com/story/news/nation-now/2016/02/21/reports-gunman-kills-least-6-michigan/80694468/.

---

[493] Ryan Felton, "Kalamazoo shooter saw 'devil.'"

[494] Emily Shapiro. "Kalamazoo Shooting Victim Testifies in Court: 'I Pretended Like I Was Dead,'" ABC News, May 20, 2016, http://abcnews.go.com/US/accused-kalamazoo-shooters-outbursts-victim-cry-hysterically-stand/story?id=39254263.

[495] Al Jones. "'He kept...shooting, shooting, shooting,' Kalamazoo victim recalls," Kalamazoo News, May 5, 2016, http://www.mlive.com/news/kalamazoo/index.ssf/2016/05/he_still_kept_shooting_shootin.html..

[496] "2016 Orlando nightclub shooting," Wikipedia. https://en.wikipedia.org/wiki/2016_Orlando_nightclub_shooting.

[497] Jack Healy. "Sitora Yusufiy, Ex-Wife of Orlando Suspect, Describes Abusive Marriage," The New York Times, June 13, 2016, http://www.nytimes.com/2016/06/14/us/sitora-yusufiy-omar-mateen-orlando-shooting.html?_r=0.

[498] Gillian Mohney. "Hostage Injured at Orlando Nightclub Recounts Hours of Pain and Fear With Gunman," Good Morning America, June 14, 2016, https://gma.yahoo.com/hostage-injured-orlando-nightclub-recounts-hours-pain-fear-000135444--abc-news-topstories.html.

[499] Joe Mozingo, Matt Pearce and Tracy Wilkinson. "'An act of terror and an act of hate': The aftermath of America's worst mass shooting," Los Angeles Times, June 13, 2016, http://www.latimes.com/nation/nationnow/la-na-orlando-nightclub-shooting-20160612-snap-story.html.

[500] Jeff Schnogol. "Marine vet's quick actions saved dozens of lives during Orlando nightclub shooting," Marinecorpstimes.com, June 14, 2016. http://www.marinecorpstime.com/story/military/2016/06/14/marine-vets-quiick-actions-saved-dozens-lives-during-orlando-nightclub-shooting/85860320/.

[501] Peter Holley and Joel Achenbach. "'It was just complete chaos': Orlando massacre survivors on the desperate struggle to stay alive," Washington Post, June 13, 2016, https://www.washingtonpost.com/news/post-nation/wp/2016/06/12/it-was-just-complete-chaos-survivors-of-orlando-massacre-recall-desperate-struggle-to-stay-alive/?utm_term=.d56268107ba1.

[502] Natalie O'Neill and Joe Tacopino. "Nightclub massacre survivors huddled in attic to stay alive," New York Post, June 12, 2016, http://nypost.com/2016/06/12/nightclub-massacre-survivors-huddled-in-attic-to-stay-alive/.

[503] (Multiple authors). "What Happened Inside the Orlando Nightclub," The New York Times, June 12, 2016. http://www.nytimes.com/interactive/2016/06/12/us/what-happened-at-the-orlando-nightclub-shooting.html?_r=0.

[504] Joe Mozingo et al. "An act of terror and an act of hate."

[505] Natalie O'Neill and Joe Tacopino. "Nightclub massacre survivors huddled in attic."

[506] Gabe Gutierrez and F. Brinley Bruton. "Dallas Gunman Micah Johnson Was 'Klutzy,' 'Goofy' While in Army," NBC News, July 13, 2016, http://www.nbcnews.com/

storyline/dallas-police-ambush/dallas-gunman-micah-johnson-was-klutzy-goofy-while-army-n608381.

507 Lauren McCaughy and Brittney Martin. "Five things you should know about Dallas shooting suspect Micah Johnson," The Dallas Morning News, July 8, 2016, http://www.dallasnews.com/news/crime/headlines/20160708-five-things-you-should-know-about-dallas-shooting-suspect-micah-johnson.ece.

508 Stephen Young, "Police Provide Details of Shootout at El Centro," Dallas Observer, July 20, 2016, http://www.dallasobserver.com/news/police-provide-details-of-shootout-at-el-centro-8504326.

509 Elahe Izadi. "How police officers protected Black Lives Matter protesters during Dallas shooting," The Washington Post, July 8, 2016, https://www.washingtonpost.com/news/inspired-life/wp/2016/07/08/the-acts-of-heroism-during-a-deadly-night-in-dallas/.

510 Ibid.

511 Joel Achenbach, William Wan, Mark Berman and Moriah Balingit. "Five Dallas police officers were killed by a lone attacker, authorities say," The Washington Post, July 8, 2016, https://www.washingtonpost.com/news/morning-mix/wp/2016/07/08/like-a-little-war-snipers-shoot-11-police-officers-during-dallas-protest-march-killing-five/.

512 Gene Johnson. "Accused Burlington mall shooter found dead in jail cell." Komo News, April 17, 2017. http://komonews.com/news/local/accused-burlington-mall-shooter-dead

513 "Court Documents: Accused mall shooter had history of violence." KOMO News and AP, September 26, 2016. http://komonews.com/news/local/accused-mall-shooter-faces-murder-charges-bail-set-at-2-million

514 Ibid.

515 Amy Held. "Accused Washington State Mall Shooter Found Dead in Jail." National Public Radio, April 18, 2017. https://www.npr.org/sections/thetwo-way/2017/04/18/524501937/accused-washington-state-mall-shooter-found-dead-in-jail

516 Hana Kim. "'I was trying to keep him alive': Survivors of Cascade Mall shooting recall night of terror, displays of bravery." Q13fox.com, November 4, 2016. http://q13fox.com/2016/11/04/survivors-show-bravery-during-cascade-mall-mass-shooting/

517 Colin Dwyer. "What We Know About the Fort Lauderdale Shooting Suspect." National Public Radio, January 7, 2017. https://www.npr.org/sections/thetwo-way/2017/01/07/508697034/what-we-know-about-the-fort-lauderdale-shooting-suspect

518 Ibid.

519 Ibid.

---

520 Lizette Alvarez, Richard Fausset and Adam Goldman. "Florida Airport Assailant May Have Heard Voices Urging Violence, Officials Say." The New York Times, January 6, 2017. https://www.nytimes.com/2017/01/06/us/fort-lauderdale-airport.html

521 Ibid.

522 "Sheriff: Fired worker killed 5, shot self as siren neared." apnews.com, June 6, 2017. https://www.apnews.com/aa7004914086421193dc201ac267d304

523 "Orlando shooting gunman kills 5 at former workplace, policy say." CBS/AP, June 5, 2017. https://www.cbsnews.com/news/orlando-shooting-multiple-fatalities-investigated-police/

524 Ibid.

525 "Sheriff: Fired worker killed 5, shot self as sired neared."

526 Emanuella Grinberg. "Something went 'incredibly wrong' with Las Vegas gunman, brother says." CNN, October 5, 2017. http;//www.cnn.com/2017/10/02/us/las-vegas-attak-stephen-paddock-trnd/index.html

527 Ken Belson, Jennifer Medina, and Richard Perez-Pena. "A Burst of Gunfire, a Pause, Then Carnage in Las Vegas That Would Not Stop." The New York Times, Oct. 2, 2017. https://www.nytimes.com/2017/10/02/us/las-vegas-shooting-live-updates.html

528 Jen Kirby and Margaret Hartman. "What we know about Las Vegas gunman Stephen Paddock." New York Magazine, October 20, 2017. http://nymag.com/daily/intelligencer/2017/10/what-we-know-about-las-vegas-gunman-stephen-paddock.html

529 Alex Dobuzinskis. "Las Vegas gunman fired on security guard before mass shooting." Aol.com, Oct. 9, 2017. https://www.aol.com/article/news/2017/10/09/las-vegas-gunman-fired-on-security-guard-before-mas-shooting/23237939/

530 Kieran Corcoran. "UPDATED: This timeline shows exactly how the Las Vegas massacre unfolded." Business Insider, Oct. 10, 2017.

531 "What We Know About Las Vegas Gunman Stephen Paddock."

532 Ibid.

533 "A Burst of Gunfire, a Pause, Then Carnage in Las Vegas That Would Not Stop."

534 Ibid.

535 Leila Fadel. "After Las Vegas Massacre, Victims Search for Their Heroes of the Night." KERA Around the Nation. http://www.npr.org/2017/10/12/557250193/after-las-vegas-massacre-victims-try-to-find-their-heroes-of-the-night

536 Stephanie Elam. "Firefighters share amazing rescue stories from Las Vegas massacre." CNN, Oct. 13, 2017. http://www.cnn.com/2017/10/13/us/las-vegas-shooting-firefighters-beyond-the-call-of-duty/index.html

537 "A Burst of Gunfire, a Pause, Then Carnage in Las Vegas That Would Not Stop."

538 "Firefighters share amazing rescue stories from Las Vegas massacre."

539 "After Las Vegas Massacre, Victims Search for Their Heroes of the Night."

---

540 Jason Hanna, Steve Almasy, Euan McKirdy and Matt Rehbein. "Source: Las Vegas shooter left behind calculations for targeting crowd." CNN, Oct. 9, 2017. http://cnn.com/2017/10/07/us/las-vegas-shooting-investigation/index.html

541 Alan Gomez and Kaila White. "Here are all the victims of the Las Vegas shooting." USA Today, Oct. 6, 2017. https://www.usatoday.com/story/news/nation/2017/10/06/here-all-victims-las-vegas-shooting/733236001/

542 Ryan Brown, Evan Perez and Shimon Procupecz, "What we know about Texas church shooting suspect Devin Patrick Kelley." CNN, November 5, 2016. http://www.cnn.com/2017/11/05/us/devin-kelly-texas-church-shooting-suspect/index.html

543 Joe Sterling. "Texas shooter's ex-wife: 'Demons...hatred' consumed him." CNN.com, Nov. 11, 2017. http://www.cnn.com/2017/11/11/us/texas-shooter-first-wife-speaks/index.html

544 Eli Rosenberg, Mark Berman, and Wesley Lowery. "Texas church gunman escaped mental health facility in 2012 after threatening military superiors." The Washington Post, November 7, 2017. https://www.washingtonpost.com/news/post-nation/wp/2017/11/07/as-texas-town-mourns-details-emerge-on-gunmans-methodical-tactics-in-church-massacre/?utm_term=.3b0971fa7be2

545 Justin Carissim and Peter Martinez. "Devin Patrick Kelley: What we know about the Texas church shooting suspect." CBS News, November 6, 2017. https://www.cbsnews.com/news/devin-patrick-kelley-texas-shooting-suspect-sutherland-springs-first-baptist-church-latest/

546 "Texas church gunman escaped mental health facility..."

547 Naomi Martin. "Grandmother died shielding grandson in Sutherland Springs church shooting." Dallas Morning News, Nov. 8, 2017. https://www.dallasnews.com/news/crime/2017/11/08/grandmother-died-shielding-grandson-sutherland-springs-church-shooting

548 Tara Fowler. "Texas church shooting survivor played dead as gunman searched for more people to shoot.' ABC News. http://abcnews.go.com/US/texas-church-shooting-survivor-played-dead-gunman-searched/story?id=50975842

549 "School shooter Nikolas Cruz: A lost and lonely killer." Sun Sentinel, February 24, 2018. http://www.sun-sentinel.com/local/broward/parkland/florida-school-shooting/fl-florida-school-shooting-nikolas-cruz-life-20180220-story.html

550 Ibid.

551 David Fleshler and Yiran Zhu. "Timeline: How the Stoneman Douglas High School Shooting unfolded." Sun Sentinel, March 9, 2018. http://www.sun-sentinel.com/local/broward/parkland/florida-school-shooting/sfl-florida-school-shooting-timeline-20180223-htmlstory.html

552 Ibid.

553 Ibid.

---

[554] Ibid.

[555] Anne Branigan. "Parkland Fla., Survivor Who Saved 20 Finally Released From Hospital." The Root, April 4, 2018. https://www.theroot.com/parkland-survivor-who-saved-20-finally-released-from-ho-1824311929?utm_source=theroot_facebook&utm_medium=socialflow

[556] "Colin Ferguson (mass murderer)," Wikipedia.

[557] "Blood stains Oregon high school," CNN, May 21, 1998. http://www.cnn.com/US/9805/21/shooting.pm/index.html.

[558] See End Note 220.

[559] See End Note 242.

[560] See End Note 320.

[561] Scott Weber. "8 Dead in Shooting at Seal Beach Hair Salon," NBC Los Angeles, October 13, 2011, http://www.nbclosangeles.com/news/local/6-Killer-in-Shooting-at-Seal-Beach-131627203.html.

[562] See End Note 395.

[563] Ibid.

[564] David Fahrenthold, Sari Horwitz, and Bill Turque. "Gunman opens fire at Colorado movie theater, killing 12," The Washington Post, July 20, 2012, http://www.washingtonpost.com/national/gunman-opens-fire-at-colorado-movie-theater-killing-12/2012/07/20/gJQA6l75yW_story_1.html.

[565] See End Note 24.

[566] "What happened inside the Orlando Nightclub," The New York Times.

[567] "Daingerfield Shooting," Cop&Cross.org., www.copandcross.org/daingerfield-shooting.html.

John Matthews is Executive Director of the Community Safety Institute (CSI) and a former Chief of Police. Matthews has been in law enforcement for more than 30 years and is a Master Police Officer with an Advanced Law Enforcement Certificate. He has a bachelor's and MBA in Administrative Management. John has worked on numerous Presidential Initiatives over the past three administrations. He is a former White House Advisor on 21st Century Policing and a Senior Advisor to the National Sheriffs' Association, and currently serves as the Director of Federal Partnerships for the National Law Enforcement Officers Memorial Fund where he leads several officer safety and wellness initiatives.

John is an award-winning writer and the author of seven books including *The Eyeball Killer*, a true crime Book of the Month and firsthand account of his capture of Dallas' only serial killer. His latest book, *Police Perspective: Life on the Beat* is an anthology of stories from his award-winning newspaper column by the same name. *Mass Shootings: Six Steps to Survival* is frequently featured on national news stories and examines four decades of these deadly crimes and presents an easy-to-remember model for survival. His books *Creating a Safer School, School Safety 101* and *Neighborhood Watch 101* focus on making our communities safer and more secure and have been the cornerstones of training programs for thousands of law enforcement officers, educators, and their community stakeholders.

John currently serves as a regular law enforcement analyst for both CNN and Fox News, providing analysis on breaking public safety stories ranging from mass shootings to terrorism and school safety, to law enforcement/community relations. For three years he was a talk show host on KRLD/CBS radio and the Texas State Network, and also hosted a safety segment on Fox 4 television. He has been featured on networks around the world and made appearances on *Good Morning America, Wolf Blitzer Reports, the Sean Hannity Show, CNN, ABC, CBS* and *NBC News, FOX News Channel, Leeza, The O'Reilly Report, Good Morning New York, Good Morning Texas, Law Enforcement Television Network, A Current Affair, Good Day Dallas, Discovery Channel*, and scores of local ABC, CBS, FOX and NBC television and radio affiliates. John's serial killer story has been featured on shows including *HBO Autopsy, Evil I, Very Bad Men, Born to Kill,* and *Murder by the Numbers*, and has been adapted by multiple network television shows.

As a Texas lawman, entrepreneur and writer, John garnered numerous awards. He was named *Outstanding Law Enforcement Officer* and awarded a Certificate of Commendation from the Texas State Senate. He received numerous awards from the Dallas Police Department including *Certificate of Merit, Life Saving Award, Certificate for Civic Achievement*, and the *Police Commendation*. He has been honored with the ACE National Education award, and both the Texas and International Downtown Association awards for building public/private partnerships. He has received three ACE National Entrepreneurship awards, an INC. 500 award, a Venture 100 award, and a Texas Press Association award for column writing.

Community Safety Institute (CSI) - For over 20 years, public safety organizations and school districts including state and national associations and the federal government have turned to the Community Safety Institute (CSI) for organizational assessments, vulnerability studies, court security audits and training, jail assessments, and staffing analysis. CSI has worked with federal, state, local and tribal public safety organizations and developed national program models which have reached thousands of organizations and tens of thousands of public safety officers.

Recognized as one of the leading public safety organizations in the country, Community Safety Institute utilizes academically sound, proven industry practices in its training, technical assistance, management assessment and evaluation initiatives. Its staff of law enforcement professionals, public safety practitioners, and academicians has completed three Presidential Initiatives, developed law enforcement training for the 2017 White House Law Enforcement Outreach Initiative, as well as a major project for the U. S. Attorney General's Office which featured the development of various assessment tools and vulnerability instruments. This report was published and distributed to law enforcement agencies nationwide to assist them in determining facility vulnerability and protecting all types of public events.

CSI is one of the country's most respected school safety organizations. The developer of the nationally known RAIN Model for classroom conflict, CSI offers over 20 school safety curriculums, has produced several national initiatives, and conducted scores of school safety audits and assessments. CSI publications include: *Creating A Safer School* (2001); *Countering Terrorism: Protecting Our Schools and Communities* (2002) and *School Safety 101* (2010, 2011, 2012 and 2018). CSI also contributed to a *Community Oriented Guide to School Safety* published by the Department of Justice (2003), and the School Crisis Response series and Pandemic Planning for Schools specifically for Education Department ERCM grantees (2005).

CSI is the developer of the Department of Justice (DOJ), SAFE School Initiative and the Schools and Universities Safety Resource Center (SUSRC) for the Bureau of Justice Assistance-funded White House School Safety Initiative (2006), founded www.UniversityCrimeWatch.org, and developed a Protecting Colleges and Universities training course. CSI's staff of law enforcement professionals,

---

educators, and academicians has developed national school safety training programs, model policies and procedures, and created a national SRO curriculum.

For more than two decades CSI has served as the primary developer of numerous law enforcement and school safety initiatives for the federal government and its public safety partners including: *Law Enforcement and Mental Health Partnerships*, the STAR Initiative, the *COPS Native American Training Series I, II, III* and *IV*, *Public Safety De-escalation Tactics for Military Veterans in Crisis* (PSDTMVC), *Public Safety De-escalation tactics for Military Veterans in Crisis* (PSDTMVC) *Trainer-of-Trainers* course, *Contracting for Public Safety Services, Cross-Deputation in Indian Country, Animal Cruelty as a Gateway to More Serious Crimes, Tribal Police and Casino Security Initiatives* project, and the *Jail Information Model*. CSI contributed to the Recently Fallen Officers and Primary Research into Law Enforcement Fatalities project for the Office of Community Oriented Policing Services (COPS); the Neighborhood Watch Toolkit, the Schools and Universities Safety Resource Center (both Presidential-directed initiatives), the *Native American Neighborhood Watch Best Practices, Human Trafficking in Indian Country, Pandemic Planning for Courts,* and *Continuity of Operations Planning* (COOP) *for Sheriffs*. CSI also served as a contributor to the VALOR and Destination Zero programs for the Bureau of Justice Assistance (BJA); Officer Safety Initiatives for the Department of Transportation; Protecting Special Events for the U.S. Attorney General's Office (USAG); Law Enforcement Leadership Training for the Bureau of Indian Affairs, Supervisory Coaching and Mentoring (BIA); Community Policing Assessments for the U.S. Parks Service, Department of Interior (DOI); the Safe School program, Youth Guns, Gangs and Drugs program, Managing Juvenile Operations and Native American Juvenile Justice program for the Office of Juvenile Justice and Delinquency Prevention (OJJDP); and multiple Weapons of Mass Destruction programs for the Department of Homeland Security (DHS) including *Jail Evacuation I, Jail Evacuation II, WMD and the Community*, and the WMD Executive level course *Managing the Incident*.

46244707R00153

Made in the USA
San Bernardino, CA
04 August 2019